FRAN
THE DA.

M000208131

FRANCES FAVIELL (1905-1959) was the pen name of Olivia Faviell Lucas, painter and author. She studied at the Slade School of Art in London under the aegis of Leon Underwood. In 1930 she married a Hungarian academic and travelled with him to India where she lived for some time at the ashram of Rabindranath Tagore, and visiting Nagaland. She then lived in Japan and China until having to flee from Shanghai during the Japanese invasion. She met her second husband Richard Parker in 1939 and married him in 1940.

She became a Red Cross volunteer in Chelsea during the Phoney War. Due to its proximity to the Royal Hospital and major bridges over the Thames Chelsea was one of the most heavily bombed areas of London. She and other members of the Chelsea artists' community were often in the heart of the action, witnessing or involved in fascinating and horrific events throughout the Blitz. Her experiences of the time were later recounted in the memoir *A Chelsea Concerto* (1959).

After the war, in 1946, she went with her son, John, to Berlin where Richard had been posted as a senior civil servant in the post-war British Administration (the CCG). It was here that she befriended the Altmann Family, which prompted her first book *The Dancing Bear* (1954), a memoir of the Occupation seen through the eyes of both occupier and occupied. She later wrote three novels, *A House on the Rhine* (1955), *Thalia* (1957), and *The Fledgeling* (1958). These are now all available as Furrowed Middlebrow books.

BY FRANCES FAVIELL

FRANCES FAVIELL

THE DANCING BEAR

With an Afterword
by John Parker

DEAN STREET PRESS
A Furrowed Middlebrow Book

A Furrowed Middlebrow Book
FM5

Published by Dean Street Press 2016

Cover by DSP
Cover painting, frontispiece drawing of Lilli Altmann, and
sketches, all by Frances Faviell

First published in 1954 by Rupert Hart-Davis Ltd.

ISBN 978 1 911413 79 0

www.deanstreetpress.co.uk

"Poor bear," they said;
"he must dance to every tune."

LILLI ALTMANN

1947

AUTUMN

1946

I

IT WAS AT the roundabout juncture of Reichsstrasse and Kaiserdamm that I first saw Frau Altmann.

Among a traffic jam of all kinds of vehicles, from Occupational cars with the British, American, French and Russian markings, to miserable horses drawing heavy wagons, the old lady was pushing a handcart. On it were piled a small wardrobe, a desk and a sewing machine. She was absurdly frail to be handling such an unwieldy thing, and her short tired legs were fighting an uneven battle with the wheels of the cart on the slight slope.

Our car was held up in the traffic, and I let down the window to see her better, for one of those sudden fogs was creeping over the whole Charlottenburg area and blotting out the gaping ruins. I noticed her distressed face, and the sweat running down it in spite of the chilly air.

When the traffic began moving again at the policeman's signal, she resumed pushing her cart, but her legs suddenly slid away under her, and the cart toppled its pyramid of furniture into the very middle of the traffic.

Picking herself up immediately she ascertained that her goods were still intact, and began trying helplessly to lift the heavy articles. Passers-by stopped to gaze curiously at her, vehicles held up by the furniture in their path began a crescendo of hooting horns and klaxons, shouts and jeers were hurled at her from every side, but no one attempted to help her as she tugged unavailingly at the sewing machine.

Our own British driver, Stampie, was not with me, the car being driven by a German who was rocking with laughter at this spectacle. Sliding back the panel of glass which separated us I said furiously, "Why don't you help her instead of laughing?"

"I!" spluttered the man, "I? Why should I help her?"

I was too angry to argue with one of a race whose complete disregard for each other shocked me, so I got out and went to the old woman's assistance.

The traffic policeman, seeing the Union Jack on the car, immediately came over, saluted me and shouted to some on-lookers to lend a hand. My driver had rather shamefacedly rushed after me, imploring me not to lift anything, and eagerly took my place. Soon there were too many helpers, and the things were piled neatly again on the cart.

I looked at the woman's face. She wasn't really so old when one was close to her, but there was a weary droop to her thin shoulders and she was breathing now in great painful gasps as she wiped her face.

She began thanking me in astonishingly good English and I asked, "Can't you get anyone to help you with these things? They are far too heavy for you."

"My son was to have come—" looking round vaguely, "I can't think what has happened to him. Fritz is a good boy."

She said this last rather defiantly as if to reassure herself, and broke off with a smile as tall lanky youth, with long un-tidy hair and a thin sullen race, came hurrying up. With a muttered greeting he pushed his mother aside and took the shafts of the cart.

"Ach! Here is Fritz! What happened to you? I was getting quite worried."

He answered sulkily, "I was kept late; why couldn't you have waited for me? You knew I would come—but no! You must go without me, and so cause all this commotion. You will be ill again, and I shall be blamed for it." He blurted this out with his face averted as if he didn't want to see me.

His mother, who had introduced herself as Frau Maria Alt-mann, turned to me, holding out her hand.

"Now all will be well, *nicht wahr*? My son will manage. Thank you a thousand times for your kind help."

"Frau Altmann," I said quietly, "you are very exhausted; let your son see to these things. Get in the car and let me drive you to your home."

As his mother hesitated the youth said firmly, "Germans are forbidden to ride in Occupational cars—the *gnädige Frau* will get into trouble." There was the faintest sneer in his voice al-though his eyes met mine squarely now.

Frau Altmann looked longingly at the car; she was trembling; the incident had unnerved her.

She said firmly, "Thank you, we haven't far to go. I will accompany Fritz, but I very much appreciate your kindness."

They went off and I got into the car again. The driver said deferentially, "Do we proceed to the Reichsstrasse now?"

"No. Follow the old lady and her son."

"Follow the old lady and her son?" he repeated maddeningly, "But why? The *gnädige Frau* will be late for her class."

"Follow them!" I said, cutting him short.

He shut the door of the car with a gesture which, although perfectly polite, showed me that in his opinion all the British were mad, and we followed the old lady and her son.

I was on my way to the Forces' Study Centre in Reichsstrasse where I was helping at the improvised school run for the British children by British Troops Berlin, and it was too early for the class which I was to take there. The face of Frau Altmann attracted me in a way I could not explain. I wanted to see more of her, and I did.

We had not gone more than two hundred metres or so when the little figure in its much too thin coat crumpled in a heap on the roadway, and this time she didn't pick herself up. My driver was out of the car as quickly as I was, the son made little objection when I told them to lift her into the car.

He gave me their address, which was quite near, and said he hoped his father would be in to admit us. He couldn't accompany us, as if he were to leave the handcart unattended for even a few minutes, everything would be stolen.

"Does your mother often faint?" I asked, for Frau Altmann was quite unconscious. He nodded. Apparently she had collapsed several times recently.

"She's not really ill," he said shortly; "she's hungry. She gives all the food to us—she won't eat herself."

We drove to the address he had given me. Number thirteen seemed an impossible dwelling at first sight. It was a large ruined house standing in what had once been a garden. The entire upper storeys had disappeared, and twisted iron girders stuck up grotesquely and helplessly against the sky. The ground floor seemed fairly intact, although it looked very shaky and the windows were covered with cardboard and the door repaired with all kinds of odd pieces of wood. It bore the number 13 clearly, and the name ALTMANN.

There was no bell, and I knocked twice. An elderly man with a calm gentle face and silver-white hair opened the door.

"Herr Altmann?"

He bowed courteously in the stiff military manner of pre-Hitler days and a look of acute anxiety came over his face when I told him that his wife was outside in my car, and could we carry her in.

"She has only fainted." I assured him, hoping that this really was the case, as we laid her on a bed in a small dark room. "It's terribly cold in here. Haven't you a stove anywhere?" I asked him as I chafed her icy hands.

I was sorry that I had asked it. I should have remembered that there was no fuel except for the Occupation before he gently told me that they had none. We covered her with some blankets and I returned to the car for my brandy flask. It was becoming all too common to see people collapsing in the streets from hunger and I always carried brandy.

She was coming to, and we poured some of the spirit between her blue lips. Presently she struggled up, protesting that she was quite all right, and trying to thank me. Her smile was the best thing I had seen on this grey and cheerless day.

I asked Fritz, who arrived with the handcart as I was about to leave, if they had anything hot to give his mother. He said that they had no fuel, but that he would go to the Grunewald and try to find some wood to light the stove.

She took both my hands in hers when I said goodbye. *"Gott wird Dick belohnen!"* she said.

I could not get her out of my mind as we drove to the Study Centre where a sergeant was waiting for me to take over his class of older boys. There appeared to be a great commotion going on in the classroom. "Shall I sit outside the door in case you want me, Ma'am?" he asked. I inquired why he thought I should need him. "They're pretty tough!" he said glumly. "Most of 'em have never had a proper tanning."

The sergeant was right. They *were* tough. And with no books, equipment or materials of any kind it taxed one's resources to keep them interested. They had arrived before the Education Authorities had made any proper arrangements for them, and the Army with a commendable lack of red tape had improvised this school for them. They came from every type of home and from various types of schools. There was only one thing they all knew, the sergeant told me, and that was father's rank.

They stood there staring curiously at me. They knew me by sight from seeing me about the school. This was the first time I had taught them.

"Sit down!" I said with more firmness than I felt. To my astonishment they sat.

I was still thinking of Frau Altmann when the sergeant told me after the class that, the Major wanted to see me in his study, and over tea I told him of the incident. He said that as I had been so impressed with her English and her face, it was possible that he could find her some teaching.

"That is, of course, providing that she wasn't an active member of the Nazi party," he added.

Somehow I didn't think Frau Altmann had been a member of any party—but one never knew. I was already learning to my surprise that there had apparently been very few Nazis anywhere. They just did not exist. If it was pointed out to the Germans that the Allies had a complete list of the party members in their possession, they would shrug their shoulders and say glibly that of course they *had* to belong, but, of course, yes, that just didn't mean a thing.

The study centre was a welcome relief from the horror of the dead ruin which was now Berlin. Troops were passing to and from classes, from the libraries, from music rooms and class rooms. They were young, healthy and astonishingly alive after the yellow-grey despairing faces in the streets. When I remarked on this to the Major he told me that few people realized what a splendid job the troops had done in Berlin during the past year.

The Berliners, having been looted, starved, cowed and raped by the Mongol Russians' conquering army, had been astounded that with the arrival of the British and Americans there had been no sackings, no shootings and no raping. Instead they had been made to help in the appalling and dreary task of restoring plumbing and drainage, and clearing up the debris left after the Battle of Berlin. The troops had worked with them, and with such a will that they had accomplished little short of miracles in the devastated city. The town was still one huge ruin—but it was now an orderly ruin, with the sewers working, the water supply restored and the lighting gradually coming back. Although it was still inadvisable to go out alone after dark, it was far safer than one could have imagined it would be a year ago.

The troops had built the large Naafi building which contained not only the shop, but various clubs and offices, as well as Military Government House on the shell of old bombed-out buildings. The U.S. troops had built the magnificent Allied Commandatura Building where Germany was now governed by the four Occupying Powers. My husband had taken me to see this, and shown me the four flag-poles with the four flags fluttering—and in the restaurant the menu in four languages, including American.

The German children, who had been little starving savages, roaming in hordes in the ruins, were now becoming human again, and this, said the Major, was also largely due to our troops who were wonderful with them. The children could be seen everywhere with the men, hanging onto their arms, riding on their backs, munching their chocolate and chewing their gum, and showing not the slightest fear, but rather a great trust in the British and American soldiers.

II

THE COMPLETE and utter devastation of Berlin had shaken me profoundly. Nothing, not even the nightmare journey from Cuxhaven across the areas of blackened and desolated towns and villages, shattered railway stations and the twisted relics of battle, had prepared one for the dead horror of this city.

As we approached the environments of Berlin our train was held up alongside a Russian one. The trucks were piled high with metal—wheels of every type—and bicycles, even children's, taps and pipes and every kind of scrap. On top of each truck sat Soviet soldiers—short stocky little Mongolian-looking men; they were peeling potatoes and with the knives occasionally scraping dirt from their filthy arms.

"All loot!" said the German train attendant dourly. "You won't see a piece of metal left in Berlin."

I reminded him of the looting Germany had done in Russia and asked if he had been in any of the German-occupied countries. He had been in Norway and in Holland, and had sent home a few things, furs and clothes, to his family.

"But that's different." he said firmly.

My little son called out to the Russian soldiers and threw some chocolate to them. They were delighted and laughingly shouted *"spasibo—spasibo!"* waving their potato knives at him.

Round Potsdam the aftermath of war was so appalling that we had coaxed our children away from the windows as we approached Berlin and the M.T.O. had come breezily down the train.

"Your journey's nearly over." he had called, "and all your good men will be waiting at Charlottenburg."

There was not a pane of glass left in the huge station from which I had been waved off by a group of gay friends in '38. Open to the rains and winds of heaven, it presented a sorry and melancholy spectacle as our train drew in. I purposely shut my eyes to the grim streets with their huge mountains of rubble and mile upon mile of yawning open ruins. Our overnight halt in Hanover, where the same appalling devastation had been made worse by the silent sullen people watching without a flicker of visible emotion the arrival in an armed convoy of the first British families, had already sickened me.

The man who drove the huge car which had met us at Charlottenburg, and whom my husband had introduced to us as "Stampie", noticed this.

"You don't want to mind about any of this," he said, waving a hand at the grey ruins and the greyer dust. "In a few days you'll be so used to it that you'll *like* them. Berlin's a grand place! I'd rather be here than anywhere else in the world, and that's a fact."

My husband had told me a lot about Stampie in his letters and on my arrival that gentleman had regarded me with a speculative eye. His look said plainly that I was on trial. Was this to be the end of good times—or was I the sort who would turn a blind eye and take him as I found him?

My small son John formed an instant liking and admiration for this hardened "old soldier" and put his hand shyly in his with the request that he might sit in front with him. Stampie had turned to me.

"Glad to have you here, M'm," he said, "and as the Boss has told you, anything you want—and I mean *anything*—just you ask Stampie. That's me, John. Everyone calls me Stampie—there's literally *nothing* I can't get you if you ask me. I know my way around."

He soon proved how true this was. In any domestic crisis one could rely on Stampie to come to the rescue with anything from a soup tureen to a clockwork train, which he provided with the minimum of trouble and expense. It was he who took me round Berlin pointing out the four sectors and all the ruins with an almost ghoulish glee until he noticed how it upset me . . . then he would suggest taking me to his Mess for a "pick-me-up" as he said.

"Doesn't it give you any satisfaction or pleasure to be riding down the Kurfürstendamm as one of the Conquering Powers?" he had asked with a quirk of one eyelid.

"None," I replied shortly—and it was true. I had come to Germany prepared to hate the Germans, wanting vengeance for the loss of many friends, and for our own Chelsea home which had been blitzed. I and my unborn son had lain in its ruins.

It was curious to find that one was filled only with horror and despair at the depths to which civilization could sink.

"I felt just the same," Stampie had agreed. "We used to cheer each other up on some of Monty's long treks with just this very thought—of riding into Berlin as a conqueror—but when we got here and saw this bloody mess and these poor devils with all the stuffing knocked out of 'em—we felt only pity."

And this from a man who had seen how the Germans had treated the civilians in the countries they had invaded and occupied. I was to find that many British soldiers, even those who had been prisoners of war under the Germans, felt pity for them.

And no one could have been quicker to exploit this innate decency and feeling for the underdog than the Germans.

We were sitting in Stampie's Mess where he had taken me after observing that I was "all in" as he described it—and no wonder, for he had conducted me on one of his sight-seeing tours which had begun with the memorial to his beloved Desert Rats and ended up with the Reichskanzlei, Hitler's headquarters, and each devastated stark ruin seemed worse than the last.

"Sorry I can't take you over Adolf and Eva's bunker," he had apologized. "We used to be able to go in—but now the Russians have taken a fancy to it we can only see it on Sundays in company with the Comrades on their conducted tours."

It was the last straw when he said ghoulishly, "There are thousands of bodies still in these ruins! But it's over a year ago now, they can't be much more than bones. When we first came the stench was awful—sweet and sickly like cancer—but it's much better now. You'll notice it sometimes after the rain though. We'll just see the Schloss now and the Dom, they both make grand ruins ..."

But I had had more than enough. The sight of this appallingly savage devastation produced a sick trembling in my stomach, a nausea so violent that I was afraid of being physically ill.

"Stop it for heaven's sake!" I had cried, and Stampie had taken a careful look at me then turned the car regretfully back through the Brandenburger Tor.

"You'll soon get used to them," was his only comment. "Why, I *like* them now."

I was puzzled when he ordered three drinks from the German bartender in his Mess, thinking that perhaps someone was to join us, but no. He put two glasses in front of himself and the third before me.

"I am honoured, M'm," he said gravely as we sat down, and he raised one of his glasses to me, "Here's to you! And a pleasant life in this old ruin, Berlin!"

We clinked glasses. I had chosen sherry, but he drank Steinhager. He lifted the second glass to himself.

"Well, here's to you, Stampie, old cock," he said, and the second Steinhager went the way of the first.

"Why do you have two?" I asked curiously.

"Oh, that's nothing. Just a habit of mine—I hate drinking alone, so I usually have two at a time and drink them in turn," he said sheepishly.

I felt he was evading my question. There had been something of a ritual in the way he had lifted the second glass. Something he didn't want to tell me about.

"You should have had brandy," he said reproachfully. "Sherry's nothing of a pick-me-up—makes me feel worse."

He had shouted this above the blare of the radio which was playing *Hörst du mein heimliches Rufen?* which, with the *Capri Fischermann* was all the rage at present in Berlin. One heard them everywhere, in every café, club and bar, just as one heard "Stardust," "Roll me over in the Clover" and the Blues.

"The last Brigadier I drove in this Horch," he told me as we turned towards Grunewald where we lived, "sat with a girl on each knee, one at his feet, and one with her feet round his neck—and all of 'em full of champagne. He took 'em all home, every one of 'em!"

I said I was glad that at least he took them home, but did Stampie mean to their homes or to his?

"Theirs!" he replied in a shocked voice. "We don't have women in our Messes here. We're not like the Yanks: they're allowed 'frats' until eight o'clock in the morning, and all the week-end if they like."

"Not," he added thoughtfully, "but what some of our chaps don't get round our rules too."

I asked if there were much fratting. He nodded. "The German girls are all right," he said firmly. "We all like them. They knock spots off the men."

The girls in the streets were strikingly attractive in spite of the lack of soap and cosmetics. Many of them stayed in bed most of the day and in the evenings went in search of the cigarettes with which to buy their food.

We were going to a French reception the evening I had met Frau Altmann, and when Stampie came to fetch us to drive us to Frohnau I told him about Frau Altmann and asked him if he would take a small parcel to her.

"Altmann," he said thoughtfully; "I knew an Altmann too, but mine doesn't live at this address—but Hermann, my friend, has relatives here in Berlin, I know."

When he fetched us after the reception he told us that he had taken the parcel, that Frau Altmann was much better. She had written me a little note which he handed me.

"She *is* a relative of old Hermann's," he said. "She's his sister-in-law . . . now isn't that extraordinary? There's old Hermann always telling me about his sister-in-law—he thinks the world of her . . . and you go and meet her like that!"

The note was written in beautiful German script.

"Sehr Geehrte Gnädige Frau," it ran, "please accept my most heartfelt thanks for your kind help yesterday. I stupidly did not ask your name. I also thank you a thousand times for the parcel of tea, milk and sugar, and the biscuits. God will show me some way to repay you.

"Maria Altmann."

I asked Stampie if she had been able to make some tea.

"They were boiling the kettle with some wood which Fritz found in the Grunewald," he replied. "I'll look in again tomorrow and see how things are. I wish you could have seen her face when she opened your parcel—she burst into tears."

I discovered afterwards that Stampie, bless him, had gone out and bought her a loaf of bread, some butter and meat from one of his many black market contacts.

"She was really starving," he said simply, when I thanked him. "I just couldn't take it. Couldn't eat my dinner for thinking of what you told me."

I asked if Fritz was the only son of the Altmanns. There was another older son missing in Russia, and two daughters, said Stampie. They were both extremely pretty, and the little one, Lilli, who danced at the Staatsoper Ballet, was a real beauty. He knew all about her from her uncle, his friend Hermann. She was a small slim blonde, absolutely nothing of her, said Stampie—looked as if a puff of wind would blow her away.

I adored ballet and had spent a lot of time drawing at rehearsals at Sadlers Wells and at the ballet in Paris. I was at once very anxious to make Lilli's acquaintance.

III

A WEEK LATER, having an hour to spare between my classes at the British school, I went to call on Frau Altmann.

There had been something I liked in her face. It wasn't anything which one could define, but something I should like to have in my face when I am an old woman. She interested me enormously, and had left an impression of goodness and integrity which was unmistakable. I wanted to see the rest of this family and get to know them.

She was busy trying to get the sewing machine to work, its fall in the street not having improved it. There was, so she said, always a lot of sewing to be done for Lilli, and Fritz had been trying to get it to work without success.

It was obvious from the welcome on her face that she was glad to see me, as she begged me to sit down. She had the most naturally perfect manners, and great dignity. There were only four chairs in the room, two of them wooden kitchen ones, the other two padded arm-chairs. All were the worse for wear, as was the cushion on the wooden box obviously used as a seat. The cardboard that took the place of glass in the windows kept out the light but not the draught.

A young girl with a pointed oval face sat on one of the wooden chairs mending a ballet shoe as I came in. Herr Altmann, who was sitting by the stove, rose hastily from his chair, as did she, and greeted me warmly.

"This is my daughter Lilli," said her mother as the young girl curtsied in the old manner and then held out her hand, "she is a dancer at the Staatsoper and must mend her shoes. You will have noticed how acute is our shoe problem in Berlin."

The hand which Lilli held out to me was so thin that one could see all the blue veins in it. Stampie was right, she was beautiful. A natural blonde, her hair was of that very rare silvery fairness which one finds in the nordic races, her eyes astonishingly dark, almost violet blue. Her young body was as straight and slim as a young sapling; too thin, for the shoulder blades stuck out sharply from the tight jersey and her breasts were almost as flat as a boy's. She wore her lovely hair drawn back severely in a ballerina's knot.

I had brought some of the almost only unrationed thing in the Naafi with me—some cakes plastered in synthetic cream and some biscuits. The stove was sulking, and Frau Altmann raked it briskly and gave an exclamation of delight as the kettle on it began to boil. They had used up all their gas ration and had no coal, and the wood which Fritz collected from the Grunewald was damp. I said I could lend them an electric kettle, but was told politely that the electricity ration was so small that it just managed for the light, if they were very careful.

She made the tea and added some of the tinned milk which I had sent in the parcel. It was luxury indeed, she said, though Lilli got a little milk sometimes in the Russian sector.

"The Russians are very good about the theatre and opera performers," said Frau Altmann.

I thought Lilli looked as if she needed a great deal of milk; she was alarmingly frail for anything so strenuous as ballet dancing.

We sat down ceremoniously at the table to drink the tea. The cups, although all odd, were of very fine old china, the lace cloth which Frau Altmann had spread on the table was of the finest kind and immaculately ironed. The tea-pot was of old family silver with their initials entwined on it, and gave me a little indication of how they must once have lived.

I tried not to see the plain hunger on their faces as Frau Altmann put the large plate of cakes on the table. She said grace, quite simply, adding, "Today we really have something to be very thankful for, haven't we, Pappi?"

A minute later Fritz burst into the room. He did not seem at all pleased to see me there, bowed stiffly, and looked round for a chair.

"I suppose I have the honour to sit on this extremely comfortable box?" he remarked in an unpleasant voice.

"You can see that all the others are occupied," said his mother serenely.

He subsided with an ill grace, took a cake and ate hungrily.

"This is the first thing I've eaten today," he said, snatching another one almost before he had finished the first.

"None of us has eaten since breakfast," said his mother mildly, "If you missed that, it was your own fault, and is it necessary to remind you, *liebling*, that we need not discuss our private affairs before a guest?"

Old Herr Altmann looked doubtfully at his untidy son and I took a careful look too. He was, like Lilli, painfully thin, his cheeks sunken and his skin dry and yellowish. He wore his hair, which was fair but darker than Lilli's, as long as did many girls. His father's, in strange contrast, was so short as to be almost shaven. Fritz's shirt, of a bright green, was open at the neck, and his dark red pullover had several stains on it. Looking at the immaculate neatness of his parents in their worn but carefully mended and pressed clothes, it didn't seem possible that they had produced this strange, restless, untidy son. Perhaps he was hungry—his eyes were never still, nor were his hands, and he had a trick of jogging his foot against the wooden box which became quite maddening.

Lilli, on the contrary, was very still as she sipped the tea which Frau Altmann had made so weak as to be almost unrecognisable. I noticed her slender hands and feet, and the grace of her thin young neck. She moved beautifully when getting up to help her mother, and I could imagine her dancing well.

We chatted of pre-war Berlin, and the present-day troubles, of the food problems and the unemployment position. They were rather guarded—they didn't know me yet, I was the wife of an Occupation official; they had to be careful. One got the impression, though, that they had all learned to be careful of their tongues, and afterwards when I knew them better I found this was so—that in the last fateful months of the war the Gestapo had been ruthless.

I liked the old people. They were well read, well informed on literature, art and music. Not on the moderns, of course, they said, as they hadn't been allowed anything foreign since the Hitler régime. They had been cut off completely, as they had been in medicine. I promised to take them some British papers and art periodicals. Lilli was very quiet, but she smiled sweetly at me several times as she resumed her shoe-mending.

Just as I was about to leave the door was flung open, there was a rush and flurry of feet, and a gay laughing girl came in, dropping things all over the place in her haste. She was of a stronger physique than Lilli, but charmingly pretty and clearly her sister. Her coat, of a pale blue angora wool, swirled round her, a gay scarf fluttered from her full throat as she glanced round for a chair, then seeing me in the one which was obviously hers, curtsied as her mother introduced her.

With her arrival the somewhat stilted conversation took on a new life. She was bursting with news and her pockets were stuffed with titbits for her family—two cigars for her father, a bag of sweets for Lilli, a packet of needles which threw her mother into exclamations of joy, and a packet of Lucky Strike cigarettes thrown neatly across to Fritz.

While she drank her tea and ate a cake for which she thanked me very charmingly in excellent but Americanized English, she made them all laugh with her account of her day's work. This was her free afternoon, she explained to me. She worked for four American gentlemen who shared a house in Dahlem. There was a cook and herself. She hadn't been there long, before that she had been employed in an American Mess, but it had been too hard. All food not consumed by members had to be burned while she and her fellow workers were starving and would gladly have eaten the wasted scraps. This was done by the order of the U.S. authorities and had nothing to do with the Mess supervisors. Some of the American men had managed to slip food out for the girls, but everything left on the tables was burned.

The four gentlemen for whom she now worked were very considerate. She was certainly not as thin as her sister and brother, and had twice as much vitality. Looking at her dancing hazel eyes and wide generous mouth I wondered just how much she was paying for all the small luxuries she brought home. As it was, her mother and Lilli kept staring at the very new-looking blue coat which looked out of place in that shabby room. Finally Frau Altmann could stand it no longer, and with an apology to me, burst out, "Ursula, where did you get that new coat?"

"Bought it, of course," replied the girl, without looking at her mother.

"But, Ursula, a coat like that costs thousands of marks."

"Well, I didn't steal it; so don't look so worried, Mutti; it'll be paid for all right."

"I suppose one of your dear Yanks gave it to you!" said Fritz nastily.

"Shut up!" snapped his sister, "and if he did, it wouldn't be any of your business. You don't mind smoking their cigarettes!"

Frau Altmann sighed and admonished them sharply. She had looked anxiously at me when Fritz made the remark about the Americans. "You must please excuse them," she apologized. "I'm afraid our nerves and our manners are not what they used to be!"

I hated the way Fritz looked at his sister Ursula, and got up to take my leave. I could hear the car at the door and knew that Stampie had come to take me to the Study Centre.

He came in at Frau Altmann's invitation and was warmly greeted by them all—even Fritz smiled and thawed a little as Stampie slapped him on the back, saying, "Well, how are things, Fritz old chap?"

They had already accepted him as one of themselves. He was an old friend of their Uncle Hermann's whom he had known apparently for several years before the war. I was curious to know how these two had first met, and meant to ask Stampie.

To Frau Altmann's joy he sat down at the sewing machine and examined it carefully.

"I can do that for you," he announced cheerfully. "Tell you what, if the Boss doesn't want me tonight, I'll come back after eight and fix it for you—I'll bring my tool bag along."

I assured him that we were staying at home for once that evening.

"Did you get this old thing from Hermann?" asked Stampie, looking up from the machine.

Frau Altmann nodded.

"I got it with the desk for Pappi and the small wardrobe for Lilli. Just fancy, Mr Stamp, I'd been hunting for a wardrobe for Lilli for such a long time, and Hermann had that one all the time!"

"He won't have much left soon if he goes on as he is now," commented Stampie dryly.

Herr Altmann sighed and explained that his brother had always been fond of the bottle. He had been a very rich and successful business man, and since he had lost everything he seemed to be finding consolation in spirits.

On the way to Reichsstrasse I learned from Stampie that Hermann was exchanging all his old family silver, porcelain and carpets for spirits. "Far better if the Russians had taken it as they did poor old Oskar's," he said. "Hermann's so keen to get drink that he's like a madman sometimes."

I asked with whom he made the exchanges. Stampie looked sheepish. "It's all right—I don't want to hear," I said hastily.

"Well—it's all wrong I know—but he takes it out on his poor wife if he can't get schnapps," he muttered.

I changed the subject. I knew from my husband that Stampie went on an occasional "blind"—and I concluded that it was probably with Hermann. Hermann had been an ardent Nazi and was waiting to get his de-nazification through before he could find employment.

"There's such a queue that Hermann'll have to wait a long time—and it's no use telling him to save up the money to pay the fine," Stampie said gloomily.

No one could be employed by the Allies until he or she had been "de-nazified." I was always hearing this word, and after the whole complicated business had been explained to me I agreed with Stampie that it was a lot of nonsense, and that anyone could just pay the fine imposed by the Court and still remain a Nazi at heart.

I had soon discovered that Stampie, although constantly chiding me for becoming upset at the misery round me and my inability to help more than a few sufferers, was himself supporting several whole families. His Black Market activities indeed were done solely for this purpose and did not benefit him at all. He could not bear to see suffering any more than I could. "Don't take on so," he would beg me; "you can't help it—there's nothing you can do."

But he always managed to do something about it himself. It was incredible to me how he achieved it, but he did, quietly and with very little fuss. I heard again and again from families whom he had helped. A Cockney born and bred, he had a wonderful gift of mimicry and would "take off" anyone. His speech varied according to his companions—from American and Australian accents he ranged to the B.B.C. "plummy" unctuousness and the clipped military speech. His German was fluent but atrocious, and delighted his friends.

He had a habit of quirking one eyebrow, indicating either amused tolerance or incredulous horror, and he was extraordinarily sensitive to one's moods. He would take a quick look at me—quirk one eyebrow and say whimsically, "Now don't take on so—come on—we'll drive to Moscow!"

There was an unfinished part of Hitler's autobahn on the Soviet border where the road ended with a barrier and a notice said, "To *Moscow*". And he would drive me there—chat with the Russian sentries, and throw them cigarettes—and make me take over the wheel.

This was strictly forbidden, but Stampie would get over that by telling me that there was nothing to stop him dropping dead at the wheel one day and where would I be if I couldn't drive the car? On the deserted and unused road, watched with interest by the Russians, I would drive and turn the unwieldy car to his satisfaction. If this failed to disperse my gloom—and it seldom did—he would invariably suggest a "pick-me-up" at his Mess, and here he would solemnly go through the ceremony of the two glasses. The second glass was, I had discovered, meant for his former Eighth Army pal Jim, whom he had left buried at El Alamein.

He was a careful and conscientious driver, and his occasional failure to turn up when most needed was due to drowning his sorrows—his married life had been unhappy—too thoroughly. This caused me on more than one occasion to be glad of the lessons he gave me on the road to Moscow.

I V

MY LITTLE SON JOHN had not settled down well in Berlin. The journey had been a shock to him and the sight of these miles of ruins seemed to bring back some memories of the Blitz. He would not sleep—being afraid that the house in which we lived would fall down in the night as had all those round us. I had sent him to the Military School in which I myself was teaching, hoping that it would distract him, but in spite of the great kindness of Frau Pfeiffer, a charming old lady in charge of the kindergarten, he was terribly unhappy there.

It was Stampie who suggested a dog to replace the one we had been obliged to leave in England. He knew a lady who had a litter of dachshunds, he said.

One afternoon on coming in from a walk in the Grunewald I was told that there was a lady waiting to see me in the salon. The woman who rose from a chair by the window and introduced herself as the Baroness B——. She was one of the most beautiful women I have ever met. A brunette, with skin of a thick camellia-like texture but with the warmth of a peach, her great dark eyes were set under a rounded childish forehead, and her full pouting mouth was exquisitely modelled under a short upper lip and a straight little nose. When she smiled she showed perfect teeth.

"I have brought the dogs," she explained, "and I have also brought my daughter Heidi."

A small plump girl with curly blonde hair, her fat legs encased in white gaiters and wearing a white fur coat, came running in at her mother's call.

Heidi curtsied to me and solemnly greeted John. "Here are the dogs, John," said the Baroness, pulling two tiny golden puppies from a capacious bag.

"The mother had five. But of course she could not feed them. There is no milk in Berlin," said the Baroness as she put the adorable little creatures down on the floor. The other three were ill. I asked what illness? "Hunger." She said simply.

I looked at the magnificent mink cape she was wearing, at her nylon stockings and at the child's fur coat. They were neither of them thin—indeed they were the first healthy-looking and well dressed Germans I had yet seen, but one never knew in this fantastic city.

She discussed the price after we had sent the children and the puppies to John's playroom. She didn't want marks. But that was nothing new. No one wanted marks if they could get cigarettes or coffee. She didn't want either of these. She wanted milk for Heidi and a pair of afternoon shoes for herself in exchange for two dogs. She had a son in the Russian Zone where he got plenty of milk in a children's home, but Heidi got no milk in the Russian sector. I asked her why her son should be in the Russian Zone. His father was a Russian colonel. He loved the child and provided everything for him. The son, Ivan, was now ten months old. Heidi was her husband's child. He was a Guards officer—she had no idea where he was now.

And the Russian colonel then, I asked, did she love him?

She looked at me with those great dark eyes and said simply, "He is a magnificent lover."

Later she asked permission to telephone to a British friend or "protector" as they were called by many German women, and to my astonishment asked for an officer whom we knew quite well, addressing him on the telephone most familiarly and telling him to pick her up later on the Hohenzollerndamm when she had left me.

"And your British friend, are you fond of him too?" I asked curiously.

She regarded me again with those heavily fringed eyes.

"He is a *much* nicer man than the Russian," she admitted, "and I like him *very* very much; but as a lover he is a failure."

She had been an actress—a serious and successful one too, but now there was work only for opera singers and ballet dancers, she explained. I asked her if she knew Lilli Altmann. I used the name under which Lilli danced. She knew her name. She was considered one of the most promising of the younger ballet corps.

"She is so light, that one," she said, "and she has looks too." I asked her if she went frequently to the opera and ballet. Her Russian friend adored both and she accompanied him several times a week.

The room was rather warm, the autumn sunshine streaming in from the lovely coloured maple trees outside the windows, and as she kept on half-pushing her fur cape from her neck I suggested that she might like to take it off as tea was coming in shortly. With a smile of thanks and an apology she flung back the cape. She was quite naked from the waist upwards. A string of lovely pearls was round her throat and a satin skirt hung loosely round her slim waist, but her two exquisitely formed breasts were quite bare.

If this were how she received her Englishman, Bill, then I could understand his collecting her in his car, although it was strictly forbidden. And the Russian colonel could hardly be blamed for having given her a son.

I had shared a cabin on the Military Ship on the way out with a woman who wore nothing at all under her dress and who kept her stockings up with garters adorned with portraits of Mr Churchill and diamond V-signs, so that this exhibition was not such a shock as it might have been. I seized the opportunity to say that I should like to paint her. Would it be possible for her to sit for me?

She was flattered, telling me that she had been painted by several artists and that she liked sitting. The difficulty would be coming into the British sector. She lived in the Russian sector with the Russian colonel. He did not like her coming into the British one—but she would see what could be done about it.

Lotte my housekeeper came hurrying back from the canteen to see that I got a square deal over the dogs, Stampie having told her that the Baroness would be coming. Her jaw dropped at the sight of the half-naked visitor. She was speechless.

We arrived at a satisfactory arrangement about payment for the dogs, but I did not like to commit myself over the milk. Milk had to be got from our American friends who were very good at helping me over desperate cases. Heidi was one of the most healthy looking children I had seen in Berlin. I told her that Lilli got a small milk ration because the Staatsoper was in the Russian sector, so why couldn't the Russian colonel get milk for Heidi?

She shrugged her bare shoulders. Heidi was the daughter of a Nazi officer; why should the Russian do anything for her? It seemed pointless to remind her that she was the wife of that same officer.

When she had gone with her mink wrap fastened over her nakedness Lotte and I laughed heartily. Neither of us had had the courage to ask her outright if she had forgotten her blouse or if it had been done deliberately to shock me.

The puppies were sweet, but after three days it was clear that they were sickening for the illness from which the remainder of the litter had died. A woman veterinary surgeon recommended by the Baroness came and pronounced that they had distemper. She admitted that the others had died of that disease. These would die too, she assured me. There were no medicines in Berlin and they were too weak already to respond to anything even if she had it.

John, who had brightened up wonderfully with the advent of the puppies, was heartbroken. I determined that these dogs should not die. Lotte and I wrapped them in old flannel nightgowns of John's and nursed them day and night. They were terribly ill with pneumonia in both lungs. The vet came again and pronounced cheerfully that both would die. Whiskey the dog would die first and Soda the bitch shortly after, she said.

I had some M and B tablets left over from John's attack of pneumonia of the previous winter, and I began giving the puppies half a tablet every two hours. The result was miraculous.

Whiskey, who had certainly been almost dying, with loud rattling breathing and a burning hot body, began to improve after two doses. Soda responded more slowly, but she did recover completely too. I could not resist telephoning that vet. She came and was astounded. She pronounced the pneumonia to be gone and begged me to give her some of this miraculous drug, but I felt guilty at having given this precious medicine to an animal when there were so many sick children needing it. My only excuse was that the tablets were rather old and I had not known that they would still be efficacious.

Stampie, who had helped in the nursing, was so indignant with the Baroness for having sold us the dogs knowing that the others had died of distemper, that he implored me not to pay for them. But when she came, as arranged, for the money and my best afternoon shoes, smiling and elegant as before, I could not resist her apologies about the poor puppies. Heidi looked like a fairy princess in her white furs. It seemed that mink and pearls were more easily obtainable in the Russian sector than soap—for the Baroness asked me for some, explaining that Bill, who usually supplied her, had used all his ration until next month.

She was a fascinating creature with the thing which we call glamour, and I determined to ask the Altmanns about her. I thought it probable that Lilli anyhow would know what kind of an actress she had been.

V

THE ALTMANNS' house lay on my route to the Study Centre, and as I went back and forth several times a day taking classes of children and troops, I got into the habit of dropping in there frequently.

The family had managed to keep quite a number of books, and I was soon reading Goethe, Heine and Schiller, and discussing them with the old people. Frau Altmann was tireless at gently correcting my German, and improving it on every possible occasion. I read Karl Haushofer's *Macht und Erde* and *Weltpolitik von Heute*, and Hans Grimm's *Volk ohne Raum*. Frau Altmann did not approve of these last, but helped me go through them, telling me in no uncertain terms her opinions of their writers. One of the things I enjoyed most was reading the German Bible with her. I took my English one and we compared them and found alternative words for the translations and in this way I learned many rare and unusual words in German.

She was, I found, devoted to her Bible and could and did find the answer to everything in it.

The whole family were avid readers and the girls in particular liked English books. Fritz, they told me, adored thrillers and detective stories.

They were intensely interested in the arts and were delighted to find that I was a painter. Frau Altmann, a deeply religious woman, was a voracious reader of theological literature in English and French as well as her own language—and yet where Fritz was concerned she was completely blind. She adored him—for her and in her eyes he could do nothing wrong, and yet she was terribly worried about him and discussed him often with me. It was his future which worried her. What was going to happen to him? Not what was going to happen to *her*, to the girls or to old Oskar, but to Fritz—always to Fritz. She told me how his whole life had been interrupted and his education ruined by his fanatical membership of the *Hitlerjugend*. During the last fantastic months before the capitulation of Germany he had been fighting in the defence of the capital. He had been barely seventeen. Since then, there had been no more schooling, nor had he shown any desire to resume his studies even if they could have found the money for the fees or the books.

One morning Stampie brought me a note from Frau Altmann. It was an invitation to a little festivity for old Oskar's birthday. The note did not tell me about the birthday; Stampie did. Herr Altmann was to be sixty-eight. I had not realized that he was so old. He was a very quiet man and talked so little about himself that I only knew he had held a very high position in a bank, and simply could not realize that he now had nothing. All his life's savings were now valueless—as were thousands of other old people's. He was always asking why they had no money from his various stocks and shares.

Stampie told me that he had evidently had a slight stroke about the time of the sack of Berlin and had never been the same since. "The poor old boy just couldn't take all those last horrors," said Stampie; "I think it turned his brain a bit."

I liked him. He was so gentle and courteous and occasionally one got a glimpse of what must have once been a brilliant mind and a calm philosophy which had not quite left him. He seemed at a loss over his strange and violent youngest offspring, Fritz, and asked me quite pathetically whether the young men in Britain were finding life so difficult. I assured him that they were finding it difficult to settle down after the war. I thought that some of Fritz's resentments and hates came from the lack of one square meal a day. He was almost six feet in height and at his age must always have been ravenous.

There were a lot of youths like Fritz going about Berlin with the same long hair, pallid faces and too bright sunken eyes. They were the German equivalent of our London "spivs." They operated in gangs from ruined houses and could be seen in the evenings at corners of Kurfürstendamm and Kaiserdamm quite openly carrying on their nefarious deals.

Fritz belonged to this type. He had no work, nor could he find any, for he refused to work for the British or the Americans. His two sisters worked hard, as did Frau Altmann. Thanks to the Major, she had several pupils now, and a small class of British children. Old Oskar was past work even if there had been any—and he kept house in the absence of the others, but what did Fritz do all day?

They were horribly poor, and always short of the barest necessities, but with the exception of Fritz they took it all as a joke and made fun of the ridiculous exchanges and "wangles" which they were obliged to engage in, to obtain some infinitesimal thing such as an onion or an apple.

I noticed that Fritz never joined in the general laughter when Frau Altmann related how she had spent an hour haggling with the grocer in exchanging a pound of flour for some dried fish which had turned out to be quite uneatable, or how she had joined a huge queue—only to find that it was to buy tickets for the afternoon's performance of *The Wonderful Box of Dr. Mabuse*.

I asked Fritz that evening, when we were all sitting round the birthday table by the light of two candles, what he did all day. On the table was a cake, baked by Frau Altmann, with Oskar written on it in melted chocolate, and I had brought a bottle of wine and some sandwiches which Lotte had made for the occasion. There was a silence when I asked Fritz this question, and I felt that it had been a tactless one.

"I live on my sisters," he said bitterly. "If I were a pretty girl as they are, or even a pretty boy, I could earn enough once or twice in a week to keep me in comfort—but, as you see, I'm just an ordinary ugly fellow—and there's no work for me."

I don't know if Frau Altmann realized the full implication of this remark, but she was very angry indeed. Her pale face flushed. "How dare you speak like that, Fritz, and in front of our guest!"

Lilli merely gave him a look which said plainly what she thought of him. I said I was sorry, that I had only asked because it was possible that we could do something to help him get employment.

"I will never work for the Occupation," he sneered.

"Then you will not get any work at all, my boy," commented his father quietly, "for everything is now under the control of the Allies; even if you are actually working under German supervision, it will be under orders from the Allied Occupation."

Fritz said that Lilli was in the Staatsoper and that it was still German.

"No it is not", she retorted with spirit. "We are entirely under Russian control really, as we would soon find out if we did not fall in with their wishes."

I asked her what she was dancing in at present. They were doing *Sadko*, which was the Russians' favourite—the troops loved it. It was very long and began early, and she would soon have to leave us. I told her that I had been to the opera the previous week, and had seen her dancing in it. Did I like it? she asked. I said that the music was enchanting, but that it had seemed more like a pantomime full of transformation scenes than pure opera, but that I liked the theme—the search for happiness.

Frau Altmann smiled. She said she preferred the more conventional operas.

"I like *Sadko* immensely," said Fritz violently; "it is full of fire, imagination, colour and movement. One gets sick of people dying all over the stage with daggers and swans." He was another person when discussing something in which he was interested, showing an intelligence and appreciation of music which were astonishing.

It was getting late—Lilli kept fidgeting and looking at the clock, but we could not open the bottle of wine and drink Pappi's health because Ursula had not come.

Frau Altmann was most punctilious about such things, and made a great ceremony of birthdays. I could see that she was uneasy herself. She went twice to the door when she thought she heard Ursula's step. She had promised to be home by five o'clock, and although untidy and careless, she usually kept her word, said her mother.

"She's probably earning another coat," said Fritz spitefully. "She doesn't get them for nothing, you know."

And just then Ursula came, as she always did, in a little flurry, and out of breath from her haste. She was apologetic as she kissed her father on the top of his head, dropping a small packet into his lap, and greeted me charmingly as she flung off her coat. There were tear-stains on her flushed face in spite of her laughter. Frau Altmann looked from the tear-stains to me meaningly, but merely signalled to Fritz to open the wine, which had been put outside the window to cool. The cake was cut, and we drank the old man's health. There was much chaffing as he untied his small gifts, for they were of a very utilitarian nature, but he was as pleased as a child with two razor-blades, some home-made cigarettes and the handkerchiefs which the girls had made and initialled from old linen.

Stampie, it seemed, had sent quite a large parcel, which they considered magnificent. I dared not think how he had acquired all the things—I had already shut my eyes to his activities. They were not really my business. He had already been engaged on them for more than a year, and I was forced to admit, as he said sheepishly, that Occupation men much higher in rank and more important than he were engaged in far more dubious traffic.

Lilli got up to go—and suddenly Ursula, who had been laughing and drinking her wine, burst into tears and told us why she was late. Things were missing from the house where she worked. One of the four Americans had missed a large quantity of cigarettes, chocolate and coffee from the cupboard in his room. The things had been bought the previous day at the U.S. Commissariat. There were only herself and the cook employed in the house. She had been kept for questioning by the four gentlemen. The things had not been found. The cook's room had been searched. Ursula slept at her mother's. They had informed the police who would shortly be arriving to search the house. The cook had insisted on this, since she herself had been searched. Ursula was obliged to warn us about it at once, although it was her father's birthday, for they would be arriving at any minute now. There was a stunned silence.

"Surely they don't think that my daughter is a thief?" whispered Frau Altmann indignantly. "We are very poor—but we haven't come down to that. We are not thieves." She put her arms round the sobbing Ursula protectively.

I got up to leave—it seemed to me that I was an intruder in this scene. The old man's face was piteous in his effort to take it all in. Just then there were two loud knocks at the door, and Fritz admitted a U.S. Military Policeman and a member of the German police. He ushered them into the room, saying loudly,

"Here are two uninvited fairies to your feast, Pappi!"

The German spoke sharply to him and, apologizing to Frau Altmann, asked if her daughter had explained matters to her.

The old lady spoke calmly and with immense dignity. "She has told me that you wish to search this house. Please look anywhere you like—you will not find any stolen goods here."

The Military Policeman, who was only a boy, looked miserably ill at ease when he saw the birthday table, the cake and the wine. He began apologizing too, saying that he had to perform his duty, however unpleasant it might be. His eyes went from Ursula's flushed, tense face to Lilli's lovely calm one and then to Fritz, who looked murderous.

"It is unnecessary to apologize—please proceed. You will need candles, we have no electricity left." Frau Altmann's placid voice was quite steady. I admired her control. The hatred on Fritz's face as he watched the two men go into the next room was appalling.

Ursula sat quite still, beside her father. I gave her a cigarette which she accepted gratefully. Frau Altmann had implored me to stay when I had again tried to leave.

I asked how many rooms they had. There were two bedrooms, one for the parents and one for the girls. Fritz slept on a divan in the sitting-room. There was the small kitchen and a bathroom. All the other rooms were too damaged to be safe. I asked Herr Altmann if the house was their own. He nodded.

"I bought it for Maria when we were first married," he said; "she loved the garden—you can't imagine what it was like. It was a beautiful garden—but now ..."

Now it was a mass of rubble and stones and pieces of iron girders. The small part they had cleared and cultivated was used for vegetables.

The police came back with Frau Altmann. They had found nothing, but they wished to search this room.

We all stood up as they looked in the two cupboards' opened all the drawers in the cabinet, and then began questioning Frau Altmann about the times of Ursula's comings and goings. I tried again to leave but she said that unless I was in a hurry she would be grateful if I would stay with her. She was so very sorry that it should have happened to spoil the *gemütlichkeit* on Pappi's birthday.

The young American M.P. asked me if the car outside was mine. I nodded, realizing that by this time Stampie would have arrived to fetch me. He seemed terribly embarrassed and said to the other policeman in atrocious German, "Come on, we're wasting our time—the things were only missed today. The girl's only just come in from her former questioning; she couldn't have got rid of them that fast."

I looked at Ursula sitting expressionless, smoking. Her face told nothing now. The German policeman was not satisfied at giving up the search so soon. He said that she could easily have handed the goods to someone in the street. The faintest flicker crossed Fritz's face as he said this. A muscle moved in that lean young jaw—or maybe I was mistaken and it was just the candlelight.

"So! You know nothing about the things? *Nein?*" insisted the German, writing in his notebook.

"I haven't the faintest idea where they are," said Ursula in perfect American.

"Answer in German, please," said the man stiffly. She repeated the words in German.

"Sign this," he commanded.

"Read it first, Ursi," shouted Fritz, "don't sign until you have read it—they're all swine and will get you *somehow!*"

"Guard your tongue!" barked the man.

She read it carefully. "He can actually write," she said shakily, and signed her name with a flourish.

The German policeman looked at the table, the wine, the cigarettes, and the old man's cigar which I had brought him.

He said slowly, "You seem to have money enough here."

Fritz started to shout something, but his mother cut him short. "It is my husband's birthday," she explained. "What we have is our own affair—our British friend here is very good to us."

I offered the man a cigarette which he accepted. I saw him look carefully at the brand as he thanked me.

"It's English, not American," said Fritz belligerently.

I offered him a lift, telling Frau Altmann that I would be expected at home—it was John's bed-time. I saw that she was near to tears. She had been disgraced in her own house on her husband's birthday. I pressed her hand and told her not to worry.

Stampie cursed all police after we had dropped the two on the Hohenzollerndamm. He hated all police—especially the Redcaps, as the Military ones were called.

"A darned shame on the old boy's birthday," he said, when I told him about it. "I'm going down there after duty tonight—I'll cheer him up a bit."

I was thinking of the expression on Ursula's face when they asked her if she knew where the missing things were, and of the flicker on that of Fritz.

I thought of how I would feel if I worked in a place where each man brought home every week great cartons containing thousands of cigarettes, worth a fortune in starving Berlin, whole cases of coffee, and box upon box containing bars of chocolate. Every tin of coffee could be sold for 500 or 600 marks, every packet of cigarettes for 200 to 250, and each small bar of chocolate for 30 marks.

Had these men who were well fed and even pampered with their snack bars and ice cream parlours open all day, in addition to their three good meals, any idea of the temptation they were putting before these starving people? Our own rations were small, but even they were worth a fortune. The private soldier was worth £25 a week on his cigarette, chocolate and soap ration alone, and one single act of immorality would provide a girl with enough cigarettes to buy her food for the rest of the week.

It was a mad, terrible world, and a very tough one here in Berlin. Girls like Lilli and Ursula could easily make money if they wished. But what if they didn't wish? Not every girl whose standards had perhaps been lowered by rape had descended to prostitution. Many had a boy friend or "regular" protector who provided the necessary cigarettes. Some girls might prefer to steal.

I saw Ursula two days later on Kurfürstendamm as I was coming out of the hairdresser's. She was wearing the blue coat, and her hair was blowing about her face; as usual she was hurrying.

I called her into the car to talk to me; it was too cold to stand about. I asked how things were.

"All right," she said. "They decided not to go on with the questioning—they called the whole thing off when the Military police began going into the question of the disposal of the rations on the Black Market. You see, I do the selling for them now. They didn't want too many questions asked—so they called it off."

"And where did the stuff really go?" I asked.

Ursula looked away then burst out angrily, "They didn't give me enough rake-off. It's a lot of trouble, and Fritz has to get his share—he passes the stuff on—they get thousands and thousands of marks. We got barely enough to buy bread and potatoes. Mutti and Pappi don't have enough food, and I'm not willing to sleep with them for a packet of cigarettes or a bar of chocolate. I'm worth more than that. I'd rather ..." Her voice trailed off.

"Steal," I said quietly. "Tell me, how did you get rid of the things so quickly?"

She said that Fritz had met her in the street at lunch-time and she had slipped the things to him. "I had noticed for some days that the cupboard was left open," she said dolefully. "Anyone could have taken the stuff, but I'm sorry now—I feel beastly—I suppose I must tell them before I'll feel any better."

I asked her how she got the coat. She looked away again, muttering that she had paid for it all right, it had been well earned. She would not look at me when I said: "So what you did to get a coat, you are not willing to do for a packet of cigarettes or a bar of chocolate—is that it?"

"That's it," she said firmly. "This coat is worth all of fifty dollars."

She had clearly worked out her own value and her own code.

"Why don't you keep up your music?" I asked, noting the misery in her young face. "Your teacher told me you are very talented."

For answer she held out her hands. They were rough, red and hard. "The cook won't do any cleaning," she said briefly; "it all falls on me."

Her logic was incomprehensible to me. If she were willing to sleep with one of the Americans for a coat, surely that same man would have paid her enough to save her from scrubbing floors and washing dishes.

"It's Mutti," she explained, a deep flush flooding her face. "She has no idea what I do. She doesn't see things as they are. I am obliged to have a daily job to satisfy her. She wouldn't believe that I earn money unless I were out at work all day. You saw how suspicious she was about the coat."

"Fritz didn't help you about that," I said drily.

"It's not his business—he's getting altogether too inquisitive," she said angrily.

She got out of the car, holding out her hand persuasively. "I guess you think I'm a slut," she smiled sadly, "and I don't know why I tell you all this—but you do understand, don't you?" Her accent was so Middle West that it was amazing. It was almost impossible to tell her from an American girl.

She was gone before I could answer, with her coat swirling round her slim legs and her hair flying in the wind.

VI

THE FIFTEENTH of November was cold, grey and miserable. A fitting day for executions. Today the Nuremberg war criminals were to be hanged, Göring, von Ribbentrop, Keitel, Rosenberg, Frank, Frick, Streicher, Jodl, Sauckel and Seyss Inquart.

I had asked the Altmanns what they thought about it. They knew me well enough to speak more freely now. Frau Altmann was quite definite that they were all war criminals and deserved death. The others were silent—even old Oskar. Frau Altmann was positive about the existence of those concentration camps without having to be shown the photographs of the revolting horrors of Belsen, Buchenwald and Ravensbruck. She had helped some very dear friends to escape one of them. Their only "crime" had been that they had a little Jewish blood in them. She had hidden them. Someone had known and had reported her. She had only just escaped being sent to one of those terrible places herself; after weeks in prison being "questioned" she had suddenly been released. She shuddered as she recalled the indignities she had suffered, and I saw Ursula look quickly at Lilli when her mother said that someone had betrayed her.

Frau Altmann said that she thought it had been criminal of the Goebbels to murder their six children. What right had any parents to take the lives of their children? I said that the Goebbels had stated that the reason for the act was that a world without the Third Reich would be a world unfit for those children to live in.

It was then that Fritz said violently that the world was in any case no fit place to live in—there was no room in it for anyone with imagination and intelligence.

"I suppose by that you mean yourself," said Ursula tartly.

Lilli said slowly, "Lots of people have thought that. It's up to you. There are plenty of ways of getting out of it."

Frau Altmann was still sighing over the Goebbels children. She had known Frau Goebbels—maybe it was that which had saved her from the concentration camp. "She was a good woman," she affirmed stoutly, "but completely under her evil husband's thumb. But they were lovely children. All the Berliners loved them. Helga, Hilde, Helmut, Holde, Helda and Heide. I knew them all—and Helmut was the sweetest. It was wicked to murder them."

Autumn was rapidly giving way to winter. The mornings and evenings were bitterly cold. Fuel was very scarce, and our radiators barely warm. But we were lucky to have any heating at all.

John had a heavy cold and Lotte had been reading to him when I reached home that day. I knew that she had been in Berlin during the siege and sacking of the city. I asked her what she thought of the hanging of the war criminals. She thought it was wrong, she said. The men had only been doing what they had been ordered to do. Germans were brought up to be obedient—and indeed she and Gisela were examples of that. They carried out orders to the letter.

I asked her what it had been like during those last weeks before the capitulation of Berlin. For answer she fetched her diary for the months of April and May 1945. I sat there reading it—and could not put it down.

I read of those last weeks during April when the Berliners realized that things were hopeless, of the broadcasts telling them that Hitler would remain in the capital and that every man must help defend it to the last; of Lotte's life with her friends in the cellars without light, water, or food; of the lack of news; of the rumours, fantastic rumours. The terrifying land torpedo, the Stalinorgel, used by the advancing Russian army pounded them ceaselessly day and night, and street-fighting going on all around them. I read of Lotte going out to forage for food—for they were starving—and of her seeing the bodies of nine young Germans, scarcely more than children, hanging from the street lamp posts. They had been hanged as deserters by the S.S. for trying to do what their leaders had already done—escape from the doomed city. On each was stuck a notice saying that he was not fit to be a German.

I read of the arrival of the attacking troops, of the looting of every watch and piece of jewellery, of the removal of every male as a prisoner, of the appalling carnage in the streets, of the mass of flesh and pieces of bodies lying all over the place, of the fires and the smoke that hung like a pall over the dying city.

The diary continued, growing in horror as it described the raping of Lotte and thousands of women—even old women of sixty-five, by the filthy Mongol troops. They were not raped once but time after time—women with their children clinging in terror to their skirts, and young women held by one man while another took his pleasure. The conquerors were drunk with spirits and with victory, and the accounts of these outrages were so revolting that I was forced to remind myself that this was a girl's diary, a diary for the year 1945. It didn't seem possible, but it was true. Every date and detail was set down in pencil—she had written it by the light of her torch— the murders of those who had tried to protect the old women:

the apology of the Russian officer who had found the bodies, his promise that the murderers would be punished, and his explanation to Lotte that the troops were mad with victory after weeks of bloody fighting and had been given forty-eight hours *Plunderfreiheit*. She had set it all down, the atrocities and the kindnesses, without comment of any kind. Just a diary. The last entry which I read was dated May 12th and said, "Today we got our first bread for weeks, baked by order of the Russians ... for which we gladly queued."

It was one of the most horrible documents I had ever read, and I felt icy cold as I put it down. Some of it was quite unprintable but I was glad that I had read it, for I felt that I understood this proud and patriotic girl better now. I appreciated her first nervousness and apprehension of me. Outwardly calm and unmoved, like thousands of other women who had been raped with appalling brutality, she was now a perfectly trained and disciplined member of my household. No one looking at her attractive face could imagine that she had endured such horrors.

I called her to me and asked if I might copy her diary. She assented, and I did so. Even as she related further horrors which she had not recorded, her face paled and she trembled violently. When I tried to comfort her, telling her that although she could never forget such an experience, time would help to take away its poignancy, she shook her head and said bitterly,

"What does it matter what happened to me—we have lost the war!"

We were looking out of the window on to the ruins of the Hohenzollerndamm. The few houses left standing were a mass of holes from the street fighting. Hardly anywhere in Berlin had a house escaped this baptism of fire.

I could now understand the strange game played by the Berlin children in the streets, which I had found our own children copying. The boys would pounce upon the girls and attempt to tear off their clothes shouting, *"Komm, Frau."*

Dr. Annemarie, my friend at the Wilmersdorf Children's Hospital, had confirmed that it was a reconstruction of what these children had seen happen to their own mothers and womenfolk during the sack of Berlin.

VII

THE WEATHER was rapidly becoming colder and accelerating the terrible hunger in the city. The thing which gripped one after the ruins was this appalling stark hunger. I had seen it in India and China, but amidst this devastation and this bitter climate it compelled one's attention more forcibly.

Children could be seen fighting viciously over the filthy scraps they managed to scavenge from the Allied dustbins. The bell was rung all day by beggars—mostly old men and women, some of them scarcely able to stand—begging for a piece of bread. It was forbidden to beg from Allied houses, but hunger made the beggars sly, and they soon knew when our Haus-meister was not about. Our Army rations delivered daily in lorries, although larger than those in England, we stretched to breaking-point trying to help some of these as well as our own staff, for whom we received no rations.

German ration cards were of five varieties according to the work done by the owner. Most women and girls, and all old people, got the "Death card", which the Germans called card number 5. The women employed in Allied households got a mid-day meal at canteens, and this induced many of them to take up household chores no matter what their former work or upbringing. Practically all women were forced to earn ciga-rettes to buy food on the black market. The younger and pret-tier the women the easier it was to earn them. Frau Altmann told me of young daughters of really good old families who slept with British and American officers for a bar of chocolate or a packet of cigarettes. She was horrified. What German man would look at them after that? she said. There were no Ger-man men for them at present. One was struck by the absence of German males between the age of nineteen and fifty-five. Hundreds of thousands were prisoners of war and millions were dead.

I commented on this and said that there was perhaps some excuse for the women. Frau Altmann looked at me as if she could not believe what I had said. There was no excuse, she said firmly. "All this new talk of sex and the teachings of Freud have done permanent harm to our womenfolk!"

"And the Nazi party?" I asked. "What has their influence been?"

She set her lips and replied that she would rather not talk about the subject, but that the harm which the Nazi party had done, not only to the women, but to the men and above all to the children, could never be remedied until God and the teachings of God were set again on their proper level in the world.

Unlike the Americans who were already on friendly terms with the Germans, we British were forbidden to be friends with them. They were not allowed in our homes, in any of our buildings, clubs, or messes. Nearly every British family had come out with introductions to German families who had relatives in England, and some of them had relatives in Berlin themselves, so that this rule was frequently broken; but its continual insistence in the mass of notices and the sheafs of rules and regulations with which we were bombarded daily made an unpleasant situation. The Americans showed much more sense in their realization that human beings cannot be kept apart by such matters as race or war.

Frau Altmann's was not the first German home I had visited since my arrival in Berlin. I frequently went to Dr Annemarie and her mother's. Dr Annemarie was on the staff of one of the largest hospitals in Berlin and through her I was able to see how terribly the children were suffering from cold and malnutrition. Besides visiting this hospital regularly, she allowed me to accompany her to the Fürsorge or Welfare Clinic for out-patients.

Her own home was always open to me and her delightful twin boy and girl and her husband all became friends of ours. She had suffered very much herself from the Nazi régime under which she had been prevented from taking her final medical degree. The advent of the Allies had opened the door to her final examinations and this post at the Children's Hospital.

Amongst the people to whom we had been given introductions from home were a couple who had been very well known and important in the Nazi world. Dr von R. had been a lawyer, and his wife a well-known hostess to the Nazi party. He was friendly and always delighted to see us when we called on them at Gatow in what had formerly been their week-end bathing hut when they had owned a yacht and spent weekends by the lake. Frau von R. remained very stiff and formal. Keeping my promise to my friends in London, I frequently took her small parcels, for she was very ill and dying slowly of cancer. She never acknowledged the parcels but placed them on a table. If she offered us coffee, it was always ersatz stuff of her own. If she offered us cakes they were ones she had baked, and sugarless. She never thanked me for anything except the visit, and she was without exception the most bitter woman I had ever met—and yet I liked her. She was honest and made no secret of her regret that the Nazi days had gone. Her husband was trying to get his de-nazification through—he had been one of the first thousand members and so would have to pay an exceptionally large fine. They were horribly poor with no income whatever; but he was utterly charming to his bitter, resentful wife.

Frau Altmann had known this couple before the war, in which Frau von R. had lost both her sons. This, combined with the shattering of her whole life, the loss of everything they possessed except the hut by the lake, and the terrible illness from which she was suffering, had all combined to make her what she now was.

"There is nothing you can do for her," Frau Altmann told me when I consulted her; "she lives in the past, longing only for the return of the Nazi glories. Her husband is more sensible, he is completely disillusioned, as he was long before the final collapse."

Whenever we went out to Gatow, where we British had a very attractive club, we passed endless queues of people trailing out to look for potatoes in the Russian Zone. There were plenty of potatoes there that winter—and in the British Zone there were none.

The *Tageblatt* recorded daily the number of deaths from hunger and cold as the winter approached. There were queues everywhere, for bread, for milk, for potatoes, for cigarettes, for cinemas, buses and trams which often never ran. We were forbidden to give lifts to Germans, but nearly everyone picked up some of these miserable starving wretches who had been waiting for hours.

There had already been food riots in Hamburg and other places in October when people had eaten thirty days' bread ration in twenty, and Sir Brian Robertson had gone there himself and ordered the ration to be increased.

At the Fürsorge I seldom saw a well-nourished child, and with the weather getting colder and colder the children's arms and legs were chapped and frost-bitten from lack of woollen clothing.

The children of school age did better. The Allies allotted them a daily ration of extra food which was distributed at the schools.

But if Berlin was a tragic city by day, at night it became a whirl of revelry. The Allies entertained on a scale which was extraordinary in a starving town, and if one went down the Kurfürstendamm or the Kaiserdamm at night every café and night club was packed with revellers. Here in these night clubs newly sprung up, Allied men and German women danced to the latest tunes from England and America as well as to contemporary German ones. All the cigarette girls came out at night. In vain did the U.S. authorities put up large posters displaying a seductive looking girl looking over her shoulder in invitation, with the caption, 'V.D. lurks in the streets'; and the British issued less blatant ones with threats of punishment to its troops—the wards of the Military Hospitals were filled with syphilis cases.

Stampie took me to some of these night clubs one evening while we were waiting for my husband who was at a stag dinner. At one of the most popular clubs, run by a woman called Sophie, we encountered Fritz and Ursula. I was astonished to

see them there. Stampie said that they often came here now
that street corners were too cold for the carrying on of their
black market activities. They were either here or at the large
café on the Reichskanzlerecke.

They were sitting in a far corner with a number of young
people. I wondered what Frau Altmann would have thought
if she could have seen them now. Fritz was flushed with wine.
He had clearly had several drinks too many—there were
bottles all over their table. His two companions, long-haired
youths like himself, were arguing loudly with him, and Ursula
was intervening angrily and obviously refusing something. She
saw us suddenly, and swept over to our table. Stampie pulled
out a chair.

"May I?" she asked me. She seemed as surprised to see me
in such a place as I had been to see her.

"Well, what do you think of our night life?" she asked,
refusing a drink from Stampie. It was obligatory to drink, and
I had chosen wine because Stampie had said that it would be
the safest: the beer was undrinkable and the spirits suspect. He
had paid for the wine with a roll of Reichmarks which had
made me stare.

"Want some?" he asked grinning. I shook my head.

"Can't get rid of 'em—and that's a fact!" he said glumly.

I knew better than to ask him how he had acquired them.
The new Military money was fetching huge prices on the
black market, as were gin, brandy and all spirits bought so
cheaply at the Naafi.

The band was playing "Tico, Tico" and the dancers, hot
and happy in the close air, were encoring it enthusiastically.

"Take a look at that girl over there" said Ursula. "She's a
man!"

The tall, dark-haired woman in the clinging white dress
showed no signs whatsoever that "she" was a man. I shook my
head in disbelief.

"It's a fact!" said Stampie. "Just as that pretty girl over there
in the pink dress is a man too."

Ursula looked to me as if she had also been drinking too
much. Her cheeks had red flags in them and her eyes were too

bright. They were extraordinary eyes and fascinated me. Two young Servicemen came in with a strapping German girl. I recognized her as the model for the nude who posed for the art class with which I helped at the Study Centre. She introduced one of the boys as her fiancé and said shyly that they were soon to be married.

I found this place quite fascinating and enjoyed it far more than the Allied receptions and dinners or the endless cocktail parties at which one met the same people every time. Stampie, however, had protested against bringing me here, insisting that the Boss'd kill him if he found out.

Ursula made no move to return to her table, and when we got up to leave I asked if we could drop her at her home. She said she would be grateful. She loathed the two youths with Fritz, she said. I asked if she were not running a terrible risk mixing with a gang of black marketeers, as she was doing. She seemed astonished and said that everyone was a gangster or a smuggler or a contact nowadays. How else did I think they could live?

She explained that her parents had no income whatsoever now, that Lilli earned just enough to keep herself alive, and that her own wages were not enough to keep the home going unless she could supplement them somehow.

There was no comment to be made. It was a moot point which was the more immoral—the black market or getting cigarettes in the way most girls got them. Ursula was apparently doing both. I remarked that Lilli looked very frail, and that when she came to pose for me she had admitted to being terribly weary. She was a delightful model and had flitted across my huge salon in a hundred lovely poses for me. I was grateful to her for having broken the evil spell which had prevented me from drawing or painting in Berlin. When she was in the room one forgot the ruins and the misery and was conscious only of transient beauty and the tantalizing inability to express it on canvas or paper.

"Lilli? She's in love," said Ursula unexpectedly. She asserted that she knew the signs and there was no doubt about it.

I said Lilli could not have much time for love. She had to dance five nights a week and rehearse most mornings.

"There are the afternoons," insisted Ursula, adding that Lilli had been coming home very late at night. There were sometimes as many as fifteen curtain-calls after the opera, so that it was natural that she should be late, but Ursula was positive that Lilli was in love—and what is more that she wasn't happy about it.

We dropped her near their ruined house. The sky was dark and stormy. There wasn't a glimmer of light from the house—and we watched her put her key in the latch and wave to us as she disappeared inside.

"Stampie," I said, "that family has got a packet of trouble coming to it."

"You've said it," he agreed, "but there isn't a darned thing we can do about it."

VIII

AT THE END of November we accompanied my husband to Brussels to an International Allied Reparations Agency Conference. Stampie drove us, and I was glad for John to have his terror of the Russians, due to the Germans' many horrific tales, completely dispersed by the charming Soviet officer at the Helmstedt checkpoint, who asked him gravely whether the toy dog he was clutching had a pass—and solemnly made one out for him. This was our first introduction to the autobahn—the Russian corridor which was later on to cause so much trouble.

In Brussels I managed to get some shoes for our staff, who were literally walking on the ground, and some ballet shoes for Lilli.

On the day after our return Stampie informed me that the Altmanns were in trouble. They had been anxiously awaiting my return as Fritz was in prison. He had got mixed up in some kind of police fracas at the Brandenburger Tor and had been in prison since the previous evening. He had gone there to meet some of his black marketeering gang and had got mixed up in a Social Democrat and Communist Meeting. The Russians having succeeded in uniting these parties, they often held demonstrations near the Tor. Fritz had somehow got arrested with a lot of other youths—and the family were terribly anxious. I said that sooner or later Fritz had been bound to get into trouble. Frau Altmann, said Stampie, was frantic. She was certain that it was all a mistake, and wanted her son got out of prison.

"And," finished Stampie, "I really believe so too—the young fool was probably listening to those smooth-mouthed speakers—not looking out for himself at all—and got caught up in the crowd."

There was nothing I could do about it until the afternoon, when I was to see the Major. I told him what had happened and asked what the procedure was about people being put in prison. He said it was a Military Government matter and gave me the names of two acquaintances at Military Government House. They were, he assured me, very helpful and extremely nice.

The major whom I saw there was non-committal, but hopeful that Fritz would be released provided that he hadn't actively resisted the police. He said he would try and find out for me, and, without promising anything, said he would do all he could.

I was doubtful about the outcome. It seemed to me that Fritz would be the first to resist if anyone laid hands on him for something he hadn't done.

On the way back I went in to tell Frau Altmann not to worry too much. She was in tears, very agitated, and could not be coaxed to eat anything. Lilli was delighted with her ballet shoes and hugged them as a child would. They fitted her perfectly and she stood poised on one toe after she had "stuffed" them with the material from her old ones. I would love to have drawn her as she stood there in that dark room. She offered to pose for me on her next free morning, and thanked me again and again.

Herr Altmann looked so cold in spite of a woollen scarf tied round his neck and pinned round his shoulders that his lips were blue and his hands dead. He was anxious about Fritz too; he didn't like it at all. The police had been to the house about Ursula and now Fritz was actually in prison. The poor old man was almost in tears. Fritz, he said, was getting very odd. He was mixed up with all kinds of people—undesirable ones. He was actually beginning to talk about the Communists as if they were not such bad people. Fancy Fritz talking like that. "He has always been violently anti-communist, a very keen member of the *Hitlerjugend*, you know," sighed old Oskar.

I said that Fritz was very young, that we all go through these strange political convictions.

"He's old enough to have more sense," said his father severely.

I asked if Ursula had been at this fracas, but was told that she had not. Frau Altmann seemed astonished at the idea. Ursula, she reminded me, had to work late. I reflected that she knew nothing of the brother and sister's activities together, and the slight smile on Lilli's face showed that she was thinking this too.

Frau Altmann was so confident that I would get her son out of prison for her that I was dismayed.

"The British are very correct," she said; "they will not hold Fritz if he is innocent. Everyone knows that the British are correct." The major at Military Government House hadn't been any too optimistic. It all depended on the charge against Fritz.

When I was getting into the car, Lilli, who had accompanied me, to thank me again for her shoes, put a hand on my arm. The cold light fell on the pale shining hair and the blue veins in her childish high forehead.

"It won't do Fritz any harm to have a taste of prison," she said looking straight at me. "He once sent someone we love terribly to prison. He's not the good boy Mutti thinks he is."

I asked what she meant, but she would not say any more; merely repeating that I should not put myself out over him.

I said that I was doing what I could because I admired her mother's fight against such hopeless odds.

"Yes," said Lilli sadly, "Mutti tries to keep us all good, she tries to get us all to church on Sundays to make us keep up our old standards of honesty. She can't bear it when we use slang or swear-words, and would be horrified if she knew . . ." she paused.

"Yes?" I asked curiously.

"Oh, nothing," breathed Lilli quickly, shivering in the cold air.

It was freezing hard and I told her to hurry in although the temperature indoors wasn't much higher than that outside.

Two days later Fritz was released. I rang up my friend at Military Government House to thank him, although I didn't know if he had helped or not. He was very casual. There had been a bunch of three youths arrested, he said. The police had been perhaps a little over-zealous; there was no charge against Fritz, who strongly denied resisting arrest, and as no one had been found who had actually seen him do so, he had been released with a warning. If I had any influence with the lad, he ended, I should tell him to watch his step. He wouldn't get off with a warning a second time.

Fritz came to thank me immediately after his release. He arrived looking much tidier than usual and brought me a bunch of lilies-of-the-valley. Knowing that they had been bought with his Black Market earnings and had cost a small fortune, I accepted them reluctantly. The money could have been better spent on food. His face wore an aggressive, resentful air, in strong contrast to the resigned hopeless look on most Germans' faces. I offered him some coffee which to my surprise he accepted.

He began thanking me rather stiffly and stiltedly for having tried to help him, adding that he would have been released anyhow eventually, as he had not committed any crime and had been wrongfully imprisoned.

I reminded him that under the Nazi regime it hadn't been necessary to have committed any crime to be thrown into prison and that he should know that. He was silent and I asked him if he missed his *Hitlerjugend*. His face lit up and lost its sullenness as he admitted that he missed it and had loved it. One had felt important, needed, respected, and of use. Now no one wanted him. There was no work except clearing away débris and even that was hard to get. No one respected him although he was anxious to get work and be of some use.

"Use to whom?" I asked.

"To Germany," he said in surprise.

His English was good but he would not work for the British, saying with an apologetic smile that he didn't like what he had seen of us, excepting present company. I understood that he had no cause to love us, but I liked his honesty and asked him to tell me what he disliked in us so much.

He said, "I don't like you politically. First I find you all hypocrites. You don't practice what you preach, and then look how you treated Mr Churchill. That great man! If he had been a German and had won the war for us he would have been showered with honours. Even as an enemy we admire him enormously, but what have you British done? You have turned him out of office—refused to have him as Prime Minister. It's unbelievable! No one can trust a nation who behaves like that."

Now, many Germans had remarked on this to me and I found it very difficult to answer.

We talked, and he was less resentful after he had eaten several large Naafi buns. The gauntness of his tall frame was terrible. He seemed to me to be looking for something to hold on to—some reed to grasp in the slough of despond into which he had fallen.

I remembered what his father had said about Communism. He was the sort of boy who filled one with despair—the kind who would snatch at any new and attractive proposition regardless of its consequences.

I asked him if the police had questioned him about his Black Market activities while he was in prison. He said scornfully that they had not. They knew all right, he said, for he and his gang had been waiting for some of the stuff to come through the Tor from the Russian Zone when the police had made their raid, mistaking some of the Social Democrats and Communists for the Black Marketeers. Most of them shut their eyes to the deals, or insisted on a cut themselves.

I warned him to be careful, telling him what the British major had said.

"Everybody does it," he said scornfully. "How could we live if we didn't?"

I X

THE TERM AT the British School would soon be ending. In the kindergarten which John attended Frau Pfeiffer had made a charming "crib" for the children. Each child had taken a toy or some small part of the whole which they had helped to build.

I had been astonished, when giving my senior drawing class the Nativity as a subject, to find that out of eighteen children between the ages of fourteen and sixteen only seven knew the story of the birth of Christ. The Major was not so astonished—he had thirty Servicemen who could not read or write.

Rules about not being friendly with the Germans were being relaxed now in so far as the children were concerned, and our authorities told us to try and help in arranging Christmas parties for German children. It was hoped that every German child in Berlin would get an invitation to an Allied Christmas party. Members of Military Government and the Control Commission alike were saving their sweet and chocolate rations to give those hungry mites an afternoon that they would remember.

I had written to the *Daily Telegraph* telling of the plight of the babies in Berlin, for I had been shown hundreds of them wrapped only in newspapers, and Dr. Gaupp of the Berlin Städtische Kinderklinik had taken me round ward after ward of children suffering from malnutrition and hunger œdema.

The response from this letter had been amazing. I had asked for old woollies and old linen for bandages, but the hundreds of parcels which began arriving through the Field Post contained all kinds of other things as well. Several British women friends willingly came and helped regularly to sort and mend the mass of clothes in these parcels, as did Frau Altmann and Frau Pfeiffer. Nothing was too much trouble for them to patch, darn and reshape. Frau Altmann indeed and

Lotte, my housekeeper, were two of my staunchest helpers in this unending work.

There were enough baby clothes in the parcels to enable us to give every child at Dr Annemarie's Fürsorge some, and we distributed them at a party to which the mothers brought them, and for which Stampie provided toys which he had bought with the sale of all his schnapps. When I remonstrated with him about this he replied, "Look—if I like to give up drinking my spirit ration and sell it—and it fetches a packet now that it's Christmas time—and with the proceeds buy some toys for these poor little blighters, well, what the hell?" And he provided a toy for every child at the party.

There were Christmas trees in almost every window; they had not been bought, but ruthlessly cut down from the lovely woods round Gatow. The Altmanns had a Christmas tree, a small one. I saw it when I called there with some gifts on my way to the Berlin Städtische Kinderklinik on Christmas Eve, or Heiligeabend as the Germans call it.

John had made friends with two little Scottish boys in our block and was now very much happier. The three of them and the two puppies had wonderful games. I dropped the three little boys at a party on my way to the Altmanns.

They were all at home and asked at once for John, who sometimes visited them with me. They wanted him to see their tree and I promised to bring him next time.

Ursula, to her mother's distress, was going out dancing with her American friend later in the evening. One didn't go out on Christmas Eve, said Frau Altmann; it was a very holy evening and one should spend it at church and in the family circle. Ursula made no comment on this. She wore a dress of a curious grey shot taffeta in which she looked extraordinarily attractive. The one lamp in the room had a pink shade and its light fell on the changing colours of the silk, so that one moment she was in rose and the next in dark blue-grey. Her mouth was painted with a gay lipstick, her nails to match. She wore nylons now and very pretty new shoes.

Lilli was huddled near the stove with an old pink woollen shawl pinned round her shoulders. She was doing nothing, and her father sat idly near her. He explained to me in his courteous way that he could not read by the very poor light. The radio was playing Christmas carols and they had all been listening—except Fritz, who was deep in a book.

Frau Altmann was concocting something on the stove, which for once was burning brightly. In spite of this the room was terribly cold. The Christmas tree was in the window on a small table; on the dining table was the Adventskranz. Red candles were burning on both.

I made my small gifts, which were placed carefully under the tree. Later on in the evening there would be the usual customary ceremony of giving and receiving, at which, said Frau Altmann pointedly, Ursula would not be present.

They had something for John and for me, said Herr Altmann; they had given the parcel to Mr Stamp, knowing that in England we usually have our presents on Christmas morning.

There was, I felt, some dissension in the air, and looking at Ursula I could see that this time it was caused by her and not by Fritz. They would be leaving the house shortly for church, said Frau Altmann, and would I accompany them? I thanked her but explained that I was on my way to the children's hospital, having promised Dr Gaupp to be present at their service that evening.

"That will be very lovely," smiled Frau Altmann; "it would have given me so much pleasure if you could have accompanied us—but you will-love the hospital service. Christmas is the most beautiful festival of the year—you love it in England as much as we do here."

I thought of those wards of sick children, that long queue of grey hollow-faced babies waiting for Dr Annemarie at her clinic, and of the poor wretches who came continually to our door for scraps, and I couldn't see that there was any joy in this Christmas. Thousands of mothers would not be able to give their children a present this year—even more would not even have a meal. What was the use of people saying that it served them right? These were not those who had made the war—one could not blame unborn babies and helpless old folk.

Perhaps Frau Altmann sensed what I was thinking, for she said, "Times are very hard for everyone—but one gets real comfort and strength from church—don't you feel that?"

There was a little silence, then Ursula said that she was not going to church—she was going out.

"But you can come to church first," said her mother. "You are not going out until later."

"What! Church before Bobbie's Bar?" jeered Fritz, looking up from his book. "I am no longer a Christian—but I draw the line at that."

"We're not going to Bobbie's Bar," said Ursula angrily; "we're going to a private party."

"Fritz is coming to church with us—if you come too, Ursula, we shall all be together—except for Kurt." Frau Altmann's voice trembled as she mentioned her firstborn in Russia.

"I am going to please you, my dear Mutti, although you know very well that I am no longer a Christian," sighed Fritz.

"He's a Communist now! That's the latest!" cried Lilli contemptuously.

"Ursula, *liebling*, you *will* come?" Frau Altmann changed the subject hastily—politics on Christmas Eve would be the last straw.

"I'm sorry, Mutti, but it's impossible."

Two red spots burned in the old lady's cheeks. "It is Heiligeabend," she said quietly, "and I am not going to spoil it by quarrelling, Ursula, but you have grieved me very much. Oskar," turning to Herr Altmann, "I think it is time you asserted your authority with your daughter."

The old man looked miserable. He adored his two girls, Lilli especially—but perhaps he realized more than his wife did that it was Ursula who kept the home going now. Herr Altmann's mind wandered a little at times, but he could still see disconcertingly clearly on occasions like this.

"Maria," he began hesitatingly, "if Ursula does not want to go to church, what is the good of worrying her? They are no longer children. Ursula is the breadwinner now—she has the right to do as she likes about it."

I said hastily that it was bitterly cold tonight with a heavy frost and that the churches were unheated, it would surely be madness to allow Lilli and her father to sit in an icy building when they could stay by a warm stove—a luxury which they so seldom enjoyed nowadays.

Frau Altmann looked at me as if I did not understand. "We always go to church on Christmas Eve," she said gently. "For you it is different, but neither Pappi nor Lilli would stay away because it is cold."

Lilli and Fritz came to the door to see me off. Fritz was strangely silent, but Lilli seemed unnaturally gay this evening. One would have thought that she was going out, not Ursula. She stood on her toes and pirouetted round the car, then suddenly kissed me shyly as I took her hand.

"Happy Christmas!" she said.

The kiss was so spontaneous that it moved me strangely. It was the first kiss I had received from a German since we came to Berlin.

Fritz was holding the car door open for me. The book he had been reading slipped from under his arm. I picked it up. It was a copy of *Das Kapital* by Karl Marx.

At the hospital in Wilmersdorf the great hall was softly lit by the candles of the huge Christmas tree. The nurses were assembled with several little convalescent patients in their arms. The hospital committee were all there with the doctors.

Gerhard, my favourite little patient, was sitting up in bed, his parents on either side of him, his eyes fixed on the shining Christmas tree adorned with the stars he had made. I remarked that he looked better.

"He is dying," said the doctor. "I doubt if he will be with us more than another week or so—but at least he has tonight with his tree and his parents."

Every ward had its little tree, and I never saw a prettier sight anywhere than those little faces lit with the candlelight, and the faces of the nurses lit by their lanterns as they sang to them from the doorways.

"*O Tannenbaum! O Tannenbaum! Wie grün sind deine Blätter!*" rang in my ears as I hurried home to my own family.

It was snowing hard when I came out of the hospital—the grim ruins were already covered. Berlin lay under a white blanket.

When I was almost home I found that I had left my notebook, with the list of families we helped regularly now, at the Altmanns'. It was still quite early, and Stampie suggested that we go home via their house as I needed the book.

The door was opened by Ursula. The others had gone to church. She asked me if I had time for a cigarette, offering me a packet of Lucky Strike. I said I had ten minutes before collecting John from his party—there were several things I wanted to ask her before Stampie came in to hurry me.

How was it, I asked her, that if she and Fritz were doing Black Market deals on a larger and larger scale, her mother had fainted from hunger the first time I had met her?

There had been debts, she explained—huge debts. They had not been "operating" for long—in fact only since she had obtained the position with the four Americans. They had suggested that she should be the "contact" for disposing of their stuff. Household jobs with the Allies, she pointed out, were much sought after for this reason now.

"I had to do it!" she said fiercely. "How would you like to have to watch your parents grow thinner and thinner and see them pretend they were not hungry so that you could eat yourself? Fritz had no work—we hadn't a penny—we were in debt to Uncle Hermann. We had been living on nothing but bread and potatoes for months. There comes a time when the stomach refuses them."

"And Fritz?" I asked. "You took him in with you?"

"I had to. Some of the gang are pretty tough, and he's tough too."

"And the coat is part of the proceeds?"

"No. Joe gave me the coat," she paused, then said bitterly: "What does it matter who it is after the Russians?"

I had heard about her experiences in the sack of Berlin. Frau Altmann had hidden both the girls on the ruined roof under the girders. Ursula hadn't stayed there. She had been raped five times.

"Why should I go to church?" she asked bitterly. "What has religion ever done for me? Mother will tell you that it was my own fault that I was raped—that it was the hand of God which saved Lilli. It was too hot and uncomfortable up on that roof—I couldn't stick it. It's all right for Lilli—she's trained to stay in uncomfortable poses. Lilli," she finished with a wry smile, "is probably the only virgin of her age in Berlin!"

"Ursula," I begged, "don't let's talk any more of these things. It's my fault for asking you—tonight's Christmas Eve. Your mother is such a good woman—she's determined to think only the best of you."

"Mutti's a saint," she agreed. "But she doesn't belong to these times any more than Pappi does. They simply can't adjust themselves to new values or to present-day life in Berlin."

I said that Fritz was reading Karl Marx and asked if he was really interested.

She thought that he was. He had several Communist friends, she said. Quite a number of the former *Hitlerjugend* were joining the new Soviet Youth movement. Fritz was looking for something better than the life he was now living. At the same time he was no longer satisfied with the small deals they were doing on the Black Market and wanted to try something really big and then quit it altogether.

"Do you think he will then join the Communists?" I asked.

She laughed—and her laugh was horrible.

"What does it matter?" she said. "Nazi, Communist or Democrat, aren't they all the same? We all want something which will give us work and fill our bellies—what does it matter if it is a Russian, British, Frenchman or American from whom I get the cigarettes? They are all men—and the British and American cigarettes are worth more—so what? Here's Joe. And he'll want his money's worth even if it *is* Christmas Eve!"

Before I could recover from this outburst a young man in the uniform of the USAF came in with her. Tall and fair, he was so loosely jointed that he seemed to be strung together with elastic. His bland young face with its short upper lip closing over perfect teeth was never still as his jaws worked chewing the eternal gum. He spoke out of the side of his mouth to avoid moving it. He was not quite sober. Ursula introduced him as "Joe" and I left them together. His arm was round her and the hot hand he had given me was already on her breast before I had left the room.

Outside the house the driver of a U.S. jeep was talking to Stampie.

"Make it snappy in there, Joe!" he called out as I came out. "It's no kind of place for a guy out here on Christmas Eve!"

He was not sober either. He lurched over to me.

"Would you care," he said coaxingly, "to do a little kissing?"

Stampie was on him like a knife.

"Would you care," he growled, "to do a little boxing? Keep a decent tongue in your head or I'll be doing something, and it won't be kissing either!"

"All right, pal—no offence meant," said the American hastily.

"He's taken a load. It'd freeze the marrow out of your bones tonight," said Stampie, who was muffled up in a kind of Balaclava helmet such as John wore.

The driver of the jeep, not at all put out, saluted me while swaying slightly. "A happy Christmas to you, Ma'am," he called.

"If it hadn't been Christmas Eve I'd have given him a happy one all right," growled Stampie.

We stopped to pick up our old Hausmeister who was trudging in the snow carrying a sack.

"Ach, it's cold!" he exclaimed as he climbed in. "And it's going to be colder, and there's no fuel in the cellars." He was delighted with some potatoes he had found and showed me a wretched little fish.

"For my cat," he said happily; "she's expecting kittens any day now, and gets a bit choosy. I'd like to give your little son one of her kittens if you will allow it."

We picked John up from his party, and his two little Scottish friends, Peter and another John, piled in with us. The lighted Christmas tree was beckoning us from our window. The snow was still falling fast, and the car made no sound on its thick carpet.

With the snow falling outside we held our tree ceremony for the staff. They had received all kinds of touching little gifts for us from some of the people we were helping. There was a little cross-stitched mat worked for me by Krista, a little girl who had been in a Russian concentration camp, and whom I was feeding, and all kinds of little parcels for John. The gift I liked best was from an old Baron who was working now at shovelling coal from the road into the Allied cellars, and whose wife was bed-ridden. He had heard I was a painter and had sent me a canvas stretcher, a mahlstick, and an instrument for removing drawing pins which had all been his own. The Altmanns' gift was a silver *bonbonnière* which I saw at a glance was valuable, and would have to be tactfully returned. It was an exquisite piece of work. The note accompanying it was signed by Maria, Oskar, Ursula and Lilli, but not by Fritz.

From him there was an envelope which contained one of the postcards now being sold all over Berlin—depicting well-known buildings, the upper portion of the card showed Berlin as it had been in 1933 at the beginning of the Third Reich, and the lower portion as it was now—a heap of ruins. Across the centre of the card in gaily coloured letters was printed, in English, "1933, Best Wishes from Berlin, 1946."

The card he had sent me was one depicting the Chancellery. On the back he had written in English,

Happy Christmas in our ruins!!!!

Fritz.

I looked at the card. Similar ones had been offered for sale by young men in the streets and they were on show in the little stationer's on Rosenecke. Were they a symbol of a race who could so advertise their maimed and shattered capital to make a little money?

What if the card were a reproduction of a water-colour made by an artist that he might eat? Could we have done the same with similar reproductions of our famous London buildings, the Temple Church for instance, destroyed by German bombs? What if they were currying favour with the Occupation by advertising thus their acknowledgment of the infamous end of that Third Reich?

I felt a certain sympathy with young Fritz, who had seen the irony and bitterness behind the gay words "Best Wishes from Berlin."

X

CHRISTMAS WAS OVER, and a terrible depression was noticeable. Everyone had done their best to ignore the growing horror of want and hunger during the festival days. Now all those small tit-bits of extra food for which people had saved for so long were all eaten, and the yellow candles had burned down to their sockets. What was there to look forward to? The bitter cold was increasing daily, there was no fuel, and the Berliners had little heart for the celebration of Silvesterabend or New Year's Eve.

The most one could hope for was that things would not get worse; no one expected them to get better. When one asked *"Wie geht es?"* the answer was always, *"Es muss gehen."*

There was a fresh spate of parties and receptions to bring in the New Year for the Occupation, given by each of the Four Powers.

Notices of deaths from hunger and cold appeared daily now in the *Tageblatt*, and on December 27th all Berlin was horrified at hearing of the arrival at the British zonal frontier of a train with 16 corpses, and 57 old people suffering so acutely from frost-bite that several more died later.

These unfortunate Germans were being forcibly sent back from Poland under the terms of the Potsdam Agreement, which stipulated however that "Germans remaining in Poland should be repatriated under humane and orderly conditions."

The humanity was remarkable by its absence, although, as one German doctor remarked to me, the dead could scarcely be described as anything but orderly.

Displaced persons were returning every day in steady streams. One met them wandering aimlessly from station to station with their miserable bundles in their frost-bitten hands, their gaunt frames in rags and utter despair in their eyes. I grew to dread having to go near any of the stations because of the impossibility of helping them all.

Coming home from a cocktail party one evening we passed a British Mess where a party was being held. The curtains were not drawn, and one could see men and women members of the Control Commission playing with balloons, pulling crackers and dancing round a large Christmas tree. Watching them outside in the snow was a group of people. One family attracted my attention. A young woman with no stockings and old felt shoes, with a shawl pinned round her weary face, held a child up to look in at the scene; two little girls clung to her skirts and tried to peep in too. Clad in rags, either of these two little mites could have posed for Andersen's little match girl. Oblivious of the bitter wind, of hunger and cold, they gazed entranced at the gaily lit scene.

Perhaps it was wrong of me to have gone in and asked them to draw the curtains. They were entitled to their party, but it was somehow unbearable that those starving people should see it.

The revellers were very decent; some of them came out and filled the children's hands with sandwiches and cakes. It was so cold that the food would quickly have frozen and the little ones stuffed the things into their clothes.

The New Year came in with the temperature dropping every day; it had not been so cold in the memory of even the very old people.

The ground was as slippery as glass. The Horch just turned round in circles on the Hohenzollerndamm, and Stampie was even paler than his nightly festivities warranted as he strove in vain to get some control on the steering wheel. We were obliged to abandon the car and get our old Hausmeister to bring buckets of ash before we could do anything. The little Volkswagens were the winners. They just sailed by, leaving all the large cars stranded.

Every day the sun melted the ice on the upper surface of the roads, and every afternoon they froze again. The snow seemed permanent under the glassy upper surface. When one went out of doors it seemed as if a thousand needles were pricking one's face. We tied up our ears and envied the Russian sentries their Balaclava helmets with slits for eyes, nose and mouth.

Stampie had been looking worried and strained for some time, and I asked him if there was anything wrong. Nothing special, he said, but it was getting more and more difficult to obtain fuel and potatoes for some of his protégés. We had deliberately shut our eyes to those bits of coal and earth from potato sacks which one could not fail to observe in the car lately. When he saw that I had noticed it, he told me that he picked up the sacks from a contact near his car unit, but that it was becoming a great worry to him. He could not bear to let his protégés down.

The previous night we had been to the Altmanns'. Lilli was at home, she wasn't well and had a hard dry cough. Frau Altmann was worried, and no wonder, for she looked terribly frail as she huddled over the stove which was so low that it was useless. The room was icy cold and the windows still unglazed. Fritz came in. He was thinner than ever, and he coughed too. They had no fuel, no one had any fuel, and the cold was becoming unbearable. Her husband felt it worse than any of them. His weak heart caused poor circulation. He was in bed, the only place where it was even moderately warm.

I asked after Ursula. She was very well, the cold seemed to suit her, said Frau Altmann drily.

"She gets plenty of food," said Fritz resentfully, "and can bear it better."

"She's a good girl," said her mother defensively, "and always brings something home for Pappi."

After I had sat there a few minutes, I was frozen. Stampie fetched in some Steinhager, which was horrible but certainly warmed one. A glass was taken to Pappi in his bed. Lilli didn't want to drink any, but Stampie coaxed her into swallowing some by telling her it would do her cough good. I didn't like the look of her, nor did Stampie.

When we were driving home he said to me, "We'll have to get some fuel for that family—or the old man and Lilli are for the high jump."

I asked how he would get it, knowing how scarce it was.

"I'll get it somehow—leave it to me," he said simply.

I said that I should like to help pay for it. He promised that I should.

The car was so cold that it was an ordeal to go out in evening dress now. It seemed fantastic that one had to dress up every night in this freezing, starving city and attend dances and dinners, but when I said so, a very important lady rounded on me sternly. It was our duty, she said, to make friends with the other Occupying Powers, and it was my duty to accompany my husband to all these official and semi-official functions.

On such a night, with the temperature almost at its lowest point that winter, a huge Ball was held in the Allied Control Administration building. Given in the month when Russia was in the "Chair", each Power taking it once in every four months, most of the honour for the arrangement of the ball fell to Russia.

It was, without exception, the most dazzling and brilliant spectacle we had ever witnessed—not excepting the most glamorous Viceregal balls in India. We danced in the huge halls of the former Kammergericht to British, Russian, French, American and German bands. The uniforms and decorations in the flag-filled and flower-scented rooms were magnificent, as were the dresses of the women. Cabaret artists flown from all over Europe performed at midnight, and the Scottish pipers thrilled everyone. People were quite frenzied in their thirst for enjoyment, their determination to have a good time at this magnificent party which had assumed the air of a real Victory Ball. I wondered what some of the German waitresses standing so demurely behind the mountains of food in their black and white uniforms and their white cotton gloves must be thinking. The cost of the flowers alone would have fed all of them. Flowers such as these indeed stood as a challenge to the right of the conqueror to luxuries—for they were all hot-house blooms grown with fuel which could have saved the lives of hundreds of old people dying daily from the cold.

As the night wore on and the small hours of the morning approached, the dancers became more and more wildly excited. Drink was in unending supply, as was food. The bands vied with each other for the popularity of their respective dance floors. At four o'clock I was fetched from the German waltz room by a wild party to hear the Four Commandants, Robertson, Clay, Koenig and Sokolowski singing the Volga Boat Song, stamping their feet in time to the music. But although a huge American friend hoisted me shoulder high the crush was so great that it was impossible to catch more than a glimpse.

Outside in the snow the sentries of the Four Powers marched smartly up and down, and the four flags fluttered in the icy air. In the deserted streets the snow gave an air of death to everything, as if the ball, still going on in the brilliantly lighted building, was a pavane for the dead of this ghost-haunted city.

An old man with a sack tied round his head was shuffling along in the gutter searching for the stubs of cigarettes which the guests might have thrown from their car windows. The driver of a cart, whose poor horse had bones almost sticking through its skin, got down and joined in the hunt. They found a stub at the same moment, and fought quite viciously in the gutter before the old man rolled over, and the driver of the cart went back to whip his poor beast. The old man sat up in the gutter and hurled filthy words at him.

At home John lay asleep. Across the bed, her arm protectively round him, lay Lotte, also asleep. Her fair hair was tangled on the pillow and she looked young and at peace. She woke up, explaining that she had got John to sleep with the greatest difficulty. He would never rest until I came home, thinking that only then was the house safe from falling down.

The following morning when I was walking with the puppies in the Grunewald, they rushed ahead and began barking madly at something under a bush. I went to investigate, and found the frozen body of an old man. He was a queer dark bluish colour, and absolutely stiff. I went back to Rosenecke where there was usually a policeman on duty. He came back with me and said it was nothing unusual, there were such bodies found every day now.

"Don't let your child out alone in Grunewald," he warned me. "There are people who would murder him for a good pair of shoes."

He knew John and me well, we passed him nearly every day on our walks.

Hunger was making many normally law-abiding citizens desperate—hunger and cold together were taking a terrible toll. At the Berlin Städtische Kinderklinik there had been a number of children brought in frozen to death. I saw these small corpses, also of a curious blue colour. Their parents had thought that the doctors could revive them. Dr. Gaupp and Dr. Annemarie and all the staff were working desperately to save children brought in in the last stages of hunger and exposure.

On January the 6th the temperature fell to minus four, or thirty-six degrees of frost. No one living in Berlin could remember such intense cold. There was no coal at all, transport was impossible on the iced roads, and we sat in our huge rooms wrapped in rugs and with hot water bottles to keep our hands from numbness. Even so, our block, having been heated until now, could not have been anything like as terrible as those permanently unheated, and Germans had neither rugs to wrap round them nor hot water bottles to help them, nor the hot cups of tea and cocoa which Lotte kept bringing us.

On this frightful morning Dr. Gaupp telephoned to know if I could obtain some penicillin to save a baby's life. Gerhard was dead, he had died just after Christmas; now she told me that my other favourite child, little Lise, had died early this morning. Death, death, death! It was nothing else. I hated the snow. It carried for me the dirge of all that is gay, coloured and vital. It brought in its white shroud the winding sheet for thousands that winter. I wanted to go home—back to London—it was almost as cold there, but people were not dying of hunger. I found myself at the piano playing Ravel's lovely *Pavane pour une Infante Défunte*, but my fingers were so numb that it was a failure.

John came in. He was muffled in jerseys and his cheeks red with cold.

"You've been crying," he accused, and put the puppies in my lap. They were cold too. Stampie found us later still huddled in blankets and trying to untie parcels with our numbed fingers.

The bell kept on being rung by our poor old beggars. Lotte kept a pot of soup constantly on the simmer, and we gave all we could a cup with a piece of bread. Many British women now brought me all their left-over bread and many little extras for those old people, as well as helping with food for the children. Had it not been for Stampie arriving I would really have given in to my despair.

He wanted some rum for old Herr Altmann, who had a very bad cold on his chest.

As I fetched the bottle I asked if they had any fuel. Yes, they still had a little of what he had managed to take them, but their electricity ration was finished and they could not use any more. Outside the Naafi building in Reichskanzler Platz there were always a gang of unfortunate people clearing away debris, guarded by police. Their only crime was that they had used more than their ration of electricity. Some of them were pitifully old to be doing such work, and it was dreadful to see such a penance.

"What you want is some of this," said Stampie; "you're all in with the cold—what about a little swig?" opening the rum bottle persuasively. I declined, but begged him to help himself. Rum agreed with him, for he asked permission to entertain John at the piano and was soon vamping a song of which he was very fond called "Why did she always say no?" and then one of his own composition, "My mother should have warned me about blondes!" He played from ear, and could remember anything once he had heard it. John adored his rollicking songs, as did the girls Lotte and Gisela. We were soon all laughing at the puppies who barked madly every time Stampie roared out the refrains.

We had a dinner party that night—and I had trouble with my staff because there were several Russian guests coming. I quite understood their reluctance to serve Russians when they had all three been raped by Russians, but I explained to them that I had to entertain the Russians as well as the French and Americans, and that if they felt they could not oblige me I would have to get other staff. Gisela had not liked serving our German guests, the von R.'s, when they had dined with us the previous week. Working for the Allies was quite another thing to waiting on Germans. I had been horrified when Frau von R. had left a tip for the staff which would have bought her an excellent dinner on the Black Market. Lotte explained to me that Frau von R. had been a great lady and that it had always been the custom to leave large tips for one's hostess's staff.

I found it even more difficult to keep my attention on Gisela's shaking hands as she served the Russian officers because of what Stampie had rushed in to tell me just before the dinner.

Fritz was in serious trouble and was on the run. I asked what the trouble was.

"This time it's pretty bad," he said glumly; "the bloody young fool took part in a food lorry hold-up on the autobahn yesterday."

The police had come upon the scene and the raiders had opened fire. Fritz had escaped, but two of the gang had been caught, and they had told the police that it was Fritz who had opened fire.

It was a criminal offence, punishable by death, for a German to be in possession of a weapon—how had Fritz got the gun?

"You'd be surprised what a racket is going on in guns as well as in every other commodity," said Stampie.

I could not ask him any more because the Russians were arriving. When going to any party, official or private, they invariably arrived *en masse*. They did not have the same lavish transport facilities as had the other three Powers, and shared conveyances. Quite high-ranking Soviet officers could often be seen in the German trams and buses, strictly forbidden to us British.

The next day I went to Frau Altmann. Stampie had told me that Herr Altmann was no better, that the cold on his chest was worse, and that they were trying to keep this new trouble of Fritz's from him. She looked pale and strained, but was overjoyed to see me, pulling me anxiously into the room and begging me to stay with her a little—she was so worried and upset that she scarcely knew what she was doing.

I didn't like the look of old Oskar at all. He was in bed muffled in blankets, with the door open between the two rooms to allow a little warmth into the freezing bedroom. The draught from the unglazed window was awful—I was surprised that the poor old man hadn't been ill before.

Frau Altmann shut the door quickly and told me she was sick with anxiety about Fritz. The police had been to the house twice the previous night, but he had not been seen. The Altmanns only knew of the incident from them. Fritz had never returned home at all.

I asked where Lilli was. She had gone out to try and get some Black Market glass for the window in Pappi's room. There was glass to be had, but it came, like everything else, from the Russian Zone, and cost a small fortune by the time it passed through so many hands. I decided to ask Stampie to get some. I knew he had a contact, for he had somehow provided glass enough to repair the greenhouses of an old friend, Heinrich, who had a nursery garden.

Lilli was coming down the street as I was leaving. She had not been able to get any glass. Stampie told her not to worry, the glass would be in that evening.

I asked about Fritz. Her mouth tightened and her eyes hardened.

"He's wanted by the police. And this time it's something awful that he's done. He's no good. What will happen now?" she cried.

She wasn't sorry for him, she said, and I found this unusual. German girls usually worship their brothers. Neither Lilli nor Ursula worshipped theirs. They both had some deep resentment against him. I asked her to come back with me so that I could give her some Ovaltine and Bovril for her father. As we were driving along the Hohenzollerndamm I thought I saw Fritz. He had his face muffled up with a scarf, but I was sure it was him.

"Stop!" I shouted to Stampie, "Look there! Isn't that Fritz?"

We slowed down and I jumped out. It was Fritz, but when he saw us he started running, and although Lilli shouted to him he disappeared among the ruins. Lilli began to cry, and I told Stampie to drive us home quickly.

"The young fool! Why can't he have the sense to face up to things?" said Stampie. "What's the use of running away?"

I reminded him that if he had really had a gun and fired at the police there would not be much chance of his getting away—they would get him somehow.

"There are ways of getting away here," said Stampie grimly, "but no one knows that he did actually have a gun yet—it's only what the police say—and you know what I think of those four-letter men!"

I took Lilli up to the flat while Stampie set about getting in touch with Hermann. She wore a black coat with a little black astrakhan cap on her shining hair. Her woollen gloves were darned in several places. She looked unutterably weary and dispirited, and sank with an exclamation of delight into an arm-chair. It was one of the days when our block was partially heated and she remarked on it, saying, "How lovely it is to be in a comfortable apartment again!"

I asked if she thought Fritz would come home.

She shook her head. She was sure he would not—she had been astounded to see him near the Hohenzollerndamm. She though he might be going to Uncle Hermann's. The police were surely watching their own house and he would not dare to come home. Her father had been too poorly to take in what the police wanted when they had come yesterday to question her mother. The doctor had forbidden him to be worried.

"Mutti always makes excuses for Fritz." she said. "She has spoilt him since Kurt has been missing. This time it won't be so easy to excuse him. If she knew what he is really like she would not be so ready to shield him."

There was something so vindictive in her usually gentle voice that I was brought up sharply by the fact that there was something I did not yet know about Fritz. I looked straight at her, but her small pointed face was a mask. "He is a Judas!" she said fiercely, becoming suffused with colour.

It was extraordinary that this child should be sitting here telling me, a stranger and an "enemy," that her brother was a Judas—but life was so fantastic here that nothing surprised me any more. She said abruptly that she must go, and I gave her the things for her father. Suddenly she burst out, "Forget what I have just said about Fritz, please. I am no better than he is!"

She cried silently for a minute, and Gisela appeared with some coffee which pulled her together. I didn't like her terrible pallor, or the blue shadows under her eyes.

I changed the subject by asking her to tell me the story of Nikki the parrot. I had seen the bracket where the parrot's cage had hung. There had been many references to Nikki, and Stampie had told me that the Russians had taken him. I asked her now, when she was sitting there cuddling Soda in her arms.

The parrot had really belonged to Fritz, she said. A friend in the Navy had brought it home to Fritz when he was quite a boy; it was one of the family. During the last few weeks of the war Fritz had been out fighting with the Home Guard defending the capital. He had rushed home frantically one day to tell them that it was all over and that they had been told to surrender to the Russians. At his mother's command he had put on his civilian clothes and hidden his uniform. It was good that he did so, for many of his friends had been taken prisoner. The two girls had been hidden up on the roof by Frau Altmann. The Russian troops had come and begun ransacking the house. They opened every cupboard and drawer and threw all the contents into the garden, when a lorry collected it. They had found Herr Altmann's wine cellar and had come back into the house very drunk. The parrot Nikki had greeted them with *"Guten Morgen!"* They had been astonished, and clustered round the cage dumbfounded. None of them had ever heard of a bird that talked. Fritz had quickly seen the advantage of this, and had made Nikki go through his entire repertoire with the exception of *"Heil Hitler."*

When one of the Russians had exclaimed, disbelieving his eyes and ears, *"niet, niet,"* the parrot had repeated the words after him. The simple men were as delighted as children, made signs that they wanted the bird, and had gone off in triumph with poor Nikki in his cage. They had not taken any more loot. Poor Nikki had saved them from losing many more possessions and from any further search for the two girls. No more troops had come, and they had been left in peace. One day one of the soldiers who had taken Nikki came to try and make them understand that they wanted food for the bird. Frau Altmann had given the man a bag of seed and written down the address where he could obtain more. Nikki was apparently well, and still a treasured possession.

As if still thinking of the incident, Lilli asked suddenly, "How much do you think nationality matters?"

I said that it depended on the person concerned—that it could nowadays be a matter of life and death—or that it did not matter at all. She said that surely as an artist I would agree that art should be international. I said that the Nazis hadn't thought so, and pointed out that she had assumed a Russian sounding name for her dancing because probably she had thought that it would help her as a ballet dancer.

"It has," she said quietly, "but not quite in the way I thought it would."

The question interested me. Here in Berlin, a city divided into four sectors by the Allies, it was impossible to avoid the question of nationality—every road traffic notice was in four languages, and one could not get away from the notices on so many buildings and bus shelters and waiting rooms. "Forbidden to Germans," "No entrance for Germans," "Not for German Use," confronted one everywhere. Frau von R. had been particularly bitter about them. Even if the Germans must be treated as pariahs, surely it was carrying things too far to refuse them shelter from the elements and the use of the lavatories at stations.

I did not think that it was this aspect of nationality with which Lilli was concerned, but a more personal one. I told her that nationality was a question which had never bothered me—that having travelled so much and mixed with so many nationalities I had found them all much the same at heart.

She was dancing that evening in *Traviata*, and had asked me to come back-stage afterwards, as the friend with whom I was going wanted to be introduced to her.

I quite forgot the Fritz affair during the opera which, beautifully staged and excellently sung, gained seventeen curtain-calls from the delighted audience. I would have enjoyed it more if the Russian officer next to me had not continually dug me in the ribs with his tommy gun in his enthusiasm. I was afraid that it might go off at any minute, One never saw them anywhere without these guns.

When we went back-stage Lilli was not there. Her friend Susi made her apologies. Lilli had fainted after the second act and had gone home.

XI

THE NEXT MORNING Stampie came to me in a great state. There had been a terrible scene at the Altmanns' last night and old Oskar was very ill indeed—he had had a stroke.

I was too astonished to say anything. He had looked the last man to have a stroke. He had seemed too quiet, too pale and too apathetic. He had certainly had a nasty cold last time I had seen him, but that was all. It was definitely a stroke, Stampie told me, and it was his second. He told me then what had happened last night.

While I had been at *Traviata*, Stampie had been at Hermann's off duty. They had been drinking, but not a lot, because the doctor had warned Hermann that if he did not go a bit slower he would soon develop cirrhosis of the liver. They had been sitting there chatting over old times when suddenly Fritz had arrived, ringing violently at the bell. He had rushed in excitedly; he was filthy and desperate.

"You must get my parents to come round here!" he shouted to Hermann. Stampie reminded him that his father was too ill with his bronchial cold to get out of bed, and said that Frau Altmann would not be able to leave him alone.

"They've got to come!" Fritz cried violently, thumping the table.

Hermann, who was at the quarrelsome stage of drinking, had flown at the boy and ordered him out of the house. He didn't want any trouble with the police, he had shouted. Fritz could damn well get himself out of the trouble, the same way as he had got into it.

Fritz guessed that the police were after him—but did not know until Stampie told him that his friends had denounced him.

"I did not fire the gun!" he insisted angrily. "It's a filthy lie! I did not open fire!"

"Will you swear to that?" Stampie asked him.

"I'll swear by anything you like!" Fritz cried, and Stampie said that he believed him.

"*I* don't believe you," Hermann said bluntly.

Fritz had become hysterical, cursing the police—both German and British—his former friends, and the Occupation, who he shouted, were to blame because he and his friends were starving. It was all their fault and especially the fault of the British. Stampie had lost his temper too and said that unless Fritz pulled himself together he would give him up to the police himself. This brought Fritz to his senses and he accepted a drink and calmed down a bit.

His uncle again ordered him out; he wanted him gone. Fritz insisted that he must see Ursula. He needed money to get away and Ursula had the money.

Stampie asked where he intended going. It was all planned, he said, but he refused to say where he was going, except that it was somewhere out of reach of the British.

"You don't need to tell me where that is, you bloody young idiot!" Stampie cried, and he had begged Fritz to give himself up and face his trial.

"I'm not going to be shot or hanged," Fritz shouted. "I haven't done anything wrong."

Hermann pointed out that the possession of a gun was a criminal offence, of which every German was well aware.

"What the hell do you mean by saying that you haven't done anything?" he cried, "It's enough that you had a gun—without taking part in an armed hold-up. Are you mad?"

Stampie saw that argument was useless. The boy was in a frightful state of nervous excitement and believed that he was being persecuted. His short spell in prison for something he hadn't done had embittered him so much that he wouldn't hear a good word about the British and screamed that they wanted to starve Germany.

Stampie, thoroughly worked up now, had roared that the Nazis hadn't bothered to feed any of the countries they had invaded. That was different, said Fritz.

Stampie said he would have handed the young fool over to the Military Police himself, had it not been that the boy trusted him implicitly in spite of his tirade against the British—and he had such a high regard for the old Altmanns. He had, as usual, plenty of money on him, but he could not bring himself to offer Fritz the means of escape—even if Fritz would have taken it. But if he could have foreseen the tragedy which ensued over the money, he would have emptied his pockets in spite of his qualms.

He was furious with Fritz for bringing this trouble on his parents. He telephoned Ursula. She agreed to meet Stampie at her parents' home in twenty minutes' time. They could not talk much on the telephone, but she absolutely refused to come to her uncle's.

Hermann, under pressure, agreed to allow his wife to give Fritz a meal. He was starving, not having eaten since the previous day, and his aunt was concerned at his appearance. Hermann was horribly afraid of the police—he didn't like this affair at all, and showed Fritz plainly what he thought of him.

Stampie found Lilli there when he reached the Altmanns'. She had come home early from the theatre, she explained; she hadn't been well. The old man was very poorly and lay in the adjacent room. Frau Altmann was nervous and tense, and Stampie had to whisper that he had seen Fritz, for old Oskar's ears were very sharp. She was horrified at his trying to escape, but said at once that she was sure he had not fired the gun— and that they had only the word of the two friends who, she said, were just wastrels. She was almost demented with anxiety about Fritz.

Ursula had arrived like a whirlwind and had behaved as furiously as one. She absolutely refused to hand over the money to Fritz. It was hers, she insisted. Fritz had taken more than his share already—she believed that he must have used it to buy the gun. She had stormed and shouted that her brother was no good, that it was useless her mother trying to talk him out of this one. She hoped he would be caught and imprisoned for a very long time.

Frau Altmann had rebuked her sharply, reminding her that her brother's life was at stake and he was still so young.

"Your own life is by no means blameless," she reminded Ursula coldly, "and I am not so easily deceived as you think."

Ursula was adamant. She would not part with the money. She would not help Fritz to escape.

"And don't you do anything to help him either!" she cried to Stampie. "He's not worth it! He is worthless!"

Her mother had ordered her to hand over the money at once.

Ursula turned on her and screamed, "You're a fool, Mother, Fritz is a filthy little traitor. Who do you think it was who betrayed you to the Gruppenleiter when you hid the Rosenthals? It was your darling Fritz! Yes! Fritz whom you adore! *Now* do you still want to excuse him?"

Frau Altmann had taken the blow between the eyes. She had looked calmly at Lilli and asked her if it were true. Her lips were trembling but she controlled herself magnificently. Lilli had nodded miserably.

"We have always known," she whispered, "but we never meant that *you* should know." She looked reproachfully at Ursula. "Ursi! How could you?" she said, and burst into tears.

At her mother's agonized expression, Ursula, already sorry for what she had done, flung herself upon her mother, crying that of course she would give Fritz the money, that she would take it to him herself.

Frau Altmann pushed her away quite abruptly.

"You should have told me, both of you," she said quietly. "Fritz was only a child—but I would have known better how to handle him had I realized how deep was his loyalty to that wretched *Hitlerjugend*."

A noise in the doorway attracted Stampie's attention. He had been wishing himself a thousand miles away from this horrible scene. They saw to their consternation that old Oskar had got out of bed. His face was flushed to a dark red and his hands shook as he tried unavailingly to speak—the words would not come out although his lips moved. Finally he burst out that he had heard everything and that Fritz was never to enter his house again. It was monstrous! Monstrous! . . . His voice rose to a scream, and suddenly he had collapsed on the floor.

When they raised him they saw that one side of his face and one arm were paralysed, and that he was muttering incoherently in a strange, slurred voice. Stampie had helped lift him back to bed, and had rushed off for the doctor. When at last he had come he had said that Herr Altmann had had a stroke, that he was dangerously ill, and must be kept absolutely quiet until they could get him into hospital.

Ursula, tight-lipped and silent now that her father was unconscious, pulled a wad of notes from her bag.

"Here's the filthy money! It's vile. Money, money, money! I never hear anything else. I hate it, *hate* it, *hate* it!" And she flung the notes on the table.

"Control yourself!" said her mother sharply. "Haven't you done enough with your shouting tonight?"

"I'll take them to Fritz," offered Stampie, jumping up.

He said the misery on Lilli's face was more than he could bear, he couldn't stand any more.

"No!" said Ursula firmly. "I will take it myself. I don't trust Fritz. He is quite capable of dragging you into this if he is caught. It would be a serious offence for you to be mixed up in helping a criminal to escape."

"He is not a criminal!" said Frau Altmann sharply. "He is just a foolish boy. Tell him to come home and face his punishment—tell him I beg him to come home."

They took the money. They saw no sign of the police, and Stampie said he was astounded. Maybe the intense cold had something to do with there being no watch on the house.

Fritz had behaved just as Stampie thought he would. He refused to go to his mother, although they told him how ill his father was. He was not risking returning to the house, he said. He had in any case to run the risk of Ursula giving him away to the police.

At this she had struck him across the face. "You little swine!" she cried. "You of all people to talk about giving people away!"

He had looked murderous, but Hermann, now completely out of patience and very drunk, had put an end to the scene.

"Get out of this house! Get out!" he had shouted so loudly that they were afraid the neighbours would hear.

Fritz went—cursing and muttering that he'd get even with everyone over this.

It was a horrible story, and poor Stampie was thoroughly upset. "Fair turned me stomach over," he said glumly, "him going off like that. Human nature can't half give you a turn."

I asked him if Fritz would really be sentenced to death if he were caught. Stampie was dubious. "The Boss'd know better than me," he said thoughtfully, "but I doubt it. He would plead hunger for the reason of the hold-up, he's very young; and the food position is giving the Allies headache enough without death sentences like that."

The Russians, he said, would make propaganda out of this sort of thing. Already there was a lot of trouble going on underground with the Communists trying to win the political battle for Berlin.

"And that's where that young idiot has gone," said Stampie dryly "He's full of Karl Marx and Wilhelm Pieck."

I asked how Herr Altmann was this morning, did Stampie know?

He was still unconscious, and had not recognized anyone in the few minutes when he had regained consciousness.

XII

FRAU ALTMANN paid me the first visit she had ever made me on the day after this scene. I was going down to see her, but Gisela announced her before I left.

She was looking terribly ill and was so agitated that she found it difficult to speak at first. She had walked, and on the frozen ground it had taken almost an hour.

Her husband was dying and she wanted Fritz back. Kurt was lost in Russia and there was no man in the house.

I couldn't see that Fritz had been anything but a worry to her—the only money he had ever brought into the house had been at the risk of police discovery—and she knew now that it was he who had betrayed her to his party and caused her imprisonment. I wondered how I would feel if John later on did such a thing to me—would I be as forgiving as she was?

I had spoken to my husband on his return about Fritz. He had been emphatic that there was nothing we could do. Fritz had chosen his own path and had burned his boats so far as returning to the British Zone was concerned.

Frau Altmann did not believe that he had gone into the Russian Zone, as we did. She had come to ask me to help her find him and make him face the police. I asked her bluntly if she had any idea where he was, but I could tell from her face that she had not.

"Isn't there some way that you can use to find him?" she begged me, "and some way in which he would be treated with leniency if he gave himself up?"

I told her that there was absolutely nothing I could do, and indeed I had again contacted my nice major at Military Government House. He had said that there was only the word of members of the gang that Fritz had been there at all—he had not been seen by the police themselves—but the fact that he had run away was proof enough that he had been concerned in the hold-up. The other youths who had given him away were now in prison awaiting charge.

I told Frau Altmann that it had really been Stampie's duty to turn him in to the police himself—but as that gentleman said, the police having been conspicuous by their absence that evening, it had served them right that Fritz had got away. Stampie did not love the police, as I knew.

Frau Altmann's face was heart-rending in its utter despair. I knew that it must have cost her a great deal to come here and plead for Fritz. I must not mind that the boy sometimes used disrespectful words and made silly remarks about the Allies, she pleaded—he was in such a muddled state that he didn't know what he was doing.

I said that I minded his open criticism and hostility far less than the sly digs and covert remarks of many others whose belts had been tightened since the end of the war.

"If I thought that it would help Fritz I would go down on my knees to you," she said, weeping in a terrible silent way.

I was obliged to tell her that it was useless. Fritz had gone—no one knew where—because of his inability to face up to his crime. She defended him as a tigress does her young, insisting that it wasn't his fault—that he had been deeply influenced by the *Hitlerjugend* in spite of all her efforts against it, that he was bitter, and felt the shame of the defeat of Germany far more than many others did.

She seemed to think that we could perhaps get a pardon for him if only he would come back. She protested passionately that Fritz could not be a Communist, as his sisters said he was. It was scarcely the time to point out that Fritz was an opportunist and would probably be just as fanatical in the Communist party as he had been in the *Hitlerjugend*, especially if he thought that the Soviet was likely to be the winner in the bitter political battle being waged for Berlin.

In the loft above the hall in our flat, I had found a number of children's toys, obviously left behind by the German family turned out when the building had been requisitioned by the British. One of these interested me very much. It was a game played with dice and small aeroplanes on a map. It was called *Wir kämpfen gegen England*, and there were all kinds of obstacles in the bomb-dropping before the aeroplane finally reached London. Stampie had brought me another one in a similar vein, and in a toy shop we had coaxed the owner to show and sell us the very latest of such games. Played on a map representing the four sectors of Berlin, it was a kind of halma with each Power playing against the other.

I fetched these now and showed them to her.

"Is it any wonder that our young people are so violent?" she said after studying them; "they are taught to kill." She told me how shocked she had been by a broadcast by the Nazi Minister for Education to Berlin schoolchildren in 1940. "God created the world," he had said, "as a place for work and battle. Whoever does not understand the laws of the battle of life will be counted out—as in the boxing ring. All the good things on this earth are trophy cups. The strong win them. The weak lose them." Fritz, Ursula and Lilli had been three of the children listening.

"I cannot understand how Fritz has become like this," she said, wiping away her tears. "I tried so hard to fight against all this Nazi teaching, and to bring them up as God-fearing, upright citizens."

"Come and look out of this window," I said, taking her by the arm.

There were seven British boys in our block—there was not one little girl. All seven, including my little son, were playing with toy pistols in the open bombed space they used as a playground. Bang! Bang! Bang! they were shouting as they took aim at each other, and one after another would fall to the ground and feign death. Useless to take away the pistols—they found more, and the endless battles went on—every day our block echoed to the Bang! Bang! Bang! and their shouts. Any kind of toy weapons were forbidden by the Allies to the German children who looked on in envy and admiration at the British ones. I felt sick suddenly—and shouted to Gisela to go and bring John in.

I remembered Stampie telling me how Monty had urged his men to learn to hate the Germans—that they had *got* to learn to want to kill them.

XIII

THERE HAD BEGUN to be cases of kidnapping by the Russians of men they needed as skilled and trained mechanics—as well as of professional men. A friend of the Altmanns' had come to me in great distress having actually seen her husband forced into a Russian lorry at the point of a gun just as she was watching him come up the road to his home after the day's work at his factory.

I took her down to Military Government House where they were very interested, but said regretfully that beyond making a protest to the Soviet authorities there was nothing they could do. The Russians, said the officer speaking to us, would simply deny the incident ever having taken place, or that they knew anything whatsoever of the man in question. His wife never saw him again.

At the Study Centre the sergeants on the teaching staff told me of three Servicemen who had disappeared when returning on the autobahn from the Zone. The second lorry travelling with theirs had missed them after some *Umleitung*, or road diversions, and they had never been seen again.

The city was a haven to those who wanted to disappear, for no one went near the dangerous roped-off buildings. The most dangerous ruins were gradually being blown up, as were the deep air-raid shelters. To destroy these shelters which housed many thousands of homeless people, because of the Disarmament Plan, added to our unpopularity. These "bunkers," as the Germans called them, were amazingly well built and planned, and many of them were almost impossible to destroy. They had saved thousands of lives, and remained standing when every other building round them had disintegrated. It seemed a pity not to be studying their manner of construction instead of depriving people of a place in which to sleep.

The cold continued without any sign of a change. In Britain they were experiencing Arctic conditions too, and the fuel question there was causing the British Government a headache. The Germans said that the Russians had imported their climate with them.

The soup kitchens were doing all they could, the *Innere Mission* and the *Heilsarmee* were doing magnificent work on practically nothing, but there were too many stomachs to feed. One went to bed with the two words, Cold, Hunger, ringing in one's ears, and awoke to them again in the morning.

It was at the Altmanns' that Stampie told us the most horrible story of hunger of this time. I had gone down to inquire for old Oskar. He was still at home—the doctor could not get him into hospital—beds were needed for those who had at least a chance of life. He lay in the cold bedroom unconscious and helpless, watched over in turn by the girls and their mother.

Ursula was quiet and tense. Lilli looked like a little ghost sitting in her favourite place by the stove, her hands clasped in her lap and her fair head bent. I sketched her as she sat there with half her face and body in shadow. We were not talking very much—the shadow of death could be sensed in the atmosphere. Ursula had told me that her mother had not spoken to her since the scene when her father had collapsed. Frau Altmann was sitting by her husband's bedside reading her Bible and watching for his slightest movement.

I closed my sketchbook—it was too poor a light to draw. Lilli asked to see the sketches and exclaimed in delight as she recognized the lovely ruined Gedächtniskirche and the Brandenburger Tor through which she passed so often on her way to the Opera House.

"I love the Gedächtniskirche as a ruin," said Ursula, leaning over Lilli's shoulder and looking too; "it was really very ugly as a building."

"Proper horror!" agreed Stampie who had just come in, having left his friend Ernie in charge of the car.

The Brandenburger Tor, which now marked the Soviet sector and from which flew the Red Flag, was his favourite sketch. "I like the old Tor," he said, "but what I'd like you to do for me one day, if it's not taking a liberty to ask you, would be a sketch of the old Desert Rats' Memorial." It was a very simple stone which marked the end of the Eighth Army's long trek, but as Stampie said, it made one think, for the names engraved on it were the ones which had been household words during the war and would be the history of tomorrow.

"Here's the history of the whole bloody war!" he had remarked when he showed it to me, "and these gaping ruins are the results of one man's mania."

"We used to walk in the Unter den Linden on Sunday evenings," sighed Lilli. "It was lovely, especially when the lime trees were in blossom, and people said that the nightingales sang there at night—Mutti has heard them."

The Unter den Linden was now one of the most desolate streets in Berlin, and the once famous limes blackened skeletons. Huge photographs of Stalin and Lenin adorned its once gay and fashionable length.

"I am very hungry," said Ursula suddenly. "I believe Mutti has forgotten that we've had no food since we came in—she's so taken up with Pappi."

Stampie pulled two large meat pies out of his capacious pocket and offered her one. She took it eagerly, breaking it in two and handing half to Lilli.

"You've had nothing all day, have you Lilli?" she asked.

"Haven't you been dancing?" I asked.

Lilli shook her head. "I had a free day today," she explained. She took the pie, but I noticed that she ate it very slowly as if it hurt her to swallow, while Ursula ate hers with the delight of a hungry child.

"When one is *very* hungry," said Lilli slowly, "the food just won't go down." She put the pie down on the table as if food nauseated her, telling Stampie sweetly that she loved it and would finish it later on.

It was then that Stampie told us his story. He had been spending the evening with a German girl who lived in a dubious house in a street off the Kaiserdamm. During the evening they heard the most terrible noise going on in the room next door—as if some very heavy person were being dragged across the room. He questioned the girl and found her peculiarly evasive and anxious to take his mind off the noise.

She used all her charms, which according to Stampie were considerable, but the sudden crash of furniture and the terrified neighing of a horse brought Stampie to his feet and had him pounding on the door from which the commotion was coming. He shouted to them to open up for the British, and when they did not obey, rushed out and fetched a Military Policeman on duty in Kaiserdamm. They were ordered to open up or a shot would be fired through the keyhole.

When at last they obeyed, Stampie and the policeman were almost sick. On the floor amidst the shambles of furniture lay a horse. It was in a ghastly state, lying in a pool of blood, an agonized expression in its eyes. It was so emaciated that its ribs stuck through its skin. The owners had used it for fetching vegetables from the market but now there were no vegetables to fetch, and nothing on which to feed the poor brute. They had no weapons, and no knives, and so they had taken the poor creature to their room so that no one should see them bludgeon it to death with chair legs.

The Military policeman was so horrified that he put a bullet through its head to end its misery. He said he would love to have put one through the couple who had done this. He and Stampie had been obliged to go outside and vomit—the mess and stench in that room were so frightful.

Nothing, said Stampie, would induce him to go near the place again. The girl, he said, knew about it, and the price of her silence had been the promise of a piece of horsemeat.

As the horrible tale came to an end I saw that Frau Altmann had come to the doorway. She shuddered as Stampie finished, but remarked that hunger did terrible things to men. I noticed that Lilli's pallor was increasing, but Ursula had gone on steadily eating her pie throughout.

"Ursula, you will go and sit with your father," said Frau Altmann. "And Lilli is to go to bed. She sat with him all the afternoon."

Ursula got up without a word, taking her pie with her.

"You will finish your food before you go to your father's bedside," said her mother sharply. "Have you no respect for the sick?"

"Poor kid! She can't do anything right in her mother's eyes," said Stampie as we went home. "The old boy is unconscious. What difference could it have made to him if she finished her food there?"

"In her mother's eyes she is the cause of her father's stroke," I said, "but she can take it—it's Lilli who can't."

"I could have kicked myself for telling that story of the horse while she was eating her pie," groaned Stampie; "I'm a thick-headed fool!"

I didn't think that I would be able to eat my dinner that evening either, but it would have been heaping coals of fire on his head to have told him so.

Herr Altmann died early next morning. Frau Altmann who had taken the late night watch had dozed off in her chair and woke suddenly to find that her husband had opened his eyes.

He had roused, tried to smile, and his lips had formed the name "Maria" before he lapsed into the coma which had ended in his death.

Stampie came to tell me, but Ursula had already telephoned me the news.

"It's a good thing the old boy has gone," said Stampie. "How could they have nursed him for long in that icy house?" He sat down heavily—he was upset at the news—but more worried at the trouble there was going to be to bury the old man. The ground was too frozen to dig graves, and Frau Altmann was absolutely determined to have her husband buried in the family plot they had bought. It might be weeks or even months before any graves could be dug if the present temperatures continued. I asked him if anyone was with the widow and if she had anyone to see to such matters for her. The pastor was there, said Stampie, and Hermann was doing all he could. His brother's death had shocked and sobered him.

Funeral arrangements seemed to have broken down completely. There were no hearses, no cars, no transport of any kind, and no mortuary space for the dead at present. Not, said Stampie, that a mortuary was necessary for Herr Altmann—the house itself being as cold as a morgue! How to get Herr Altmann to his last resting place was the problem.

Was there any news of Fritz? I asked, not having liked to upset Frau Altmann the previous evening by mentioning him.

"None," said Stampie. "He's well away by now—I don't believe he's still in Berlin, although his mother does."

XIV

STAMPIE'S FEARS proved only too true. Coffins were terribly expensive and very difficult to obtain. Wood was at a premium for fuel. Many people had burned pieces of furniture and torn up their parquet flooring to get a little warmth.

No one could be found with either the strength or the will to dig graves, until the thaw set in. Short of blasting the ground for a grave, Stampie said, there was no means of getting one. There were some mass graves which the Allies had ordered to be dug in case of epidemics the previous year and the suggestion was to bury Herr Altmann in one of these and transfer him later on to his own plot.

Frau Altmann was horrified; she could not bear the idea; to her it was heathenish. Ursula, when I saw her the following morning, told me bluntly that she was sick of the whole question, and considered her mother most unreasonable. "She just won't realize that times are not normal," she complained. "Pappi is dead, and really it's better for him. He could not get accustomed to this new way of life—he was too old and tired. What does it matter where he is buried? He is out of it all."

She was impatient at all the fuss going on at home. Her Aunt Luise was with her mother and several friends. They did nothing but talk and weep. She was tired of it. Pappi had been dead for three days now and still there was nothing settled about the funeral, but she and Lilli had to go on working and the household had to go on running.

Ursula looked extremely attractive on this winter morning. As her mother had said, the cold seemed to suit her. She hadn't the same flawless skin as her sister Lilli and her mother had, but a film of make-up did wonders for her. She wore a black coat which looked new, but which she told me was her aunt's, and her hair curling all up over her cap seemed alive with vitality. The cold light from the snow which was not flattering to most women did lovely things to Ursula. The colour in her high cheekbones may have come from Max Factor or from nature, the long lashes had been darkened and swept disturbingly over them. Her wide mouth was painted a dark crimson. She was amazingly attractive. The Allied influence on the German women, who had not been encouraged to use cosmetics before, was already visible, and these commodities were fetching fantastic prices on the Black Market.

I inquired how Lilli was. I knew that she had taken her father's death very hard. She was his favourite. She was disturbingly quiet, said Ursula. Her mother, she thought, was grieving just as much about Fritz as about her father—and please wouldn't I come and see her?

They missed Fritz, she admitted. He had been a nuisance and he ate a great deal, but he was provocative. One had never been dull when he was around.

She looked anything but dull herself. I found her extraordinarily interesting and I asked how Joe was. He was, she said, tossing her lovely hair out of her eyes, absolutely crazy about her now—and becoming very jealous. It seemed to amuse her. There was no longer any question of her having to earn cigarettes from anyone else. He supplied all her needs. "In fact I've got me a regular," she said laughing.

I said it must be much easier and pleasanter that way and I was glad. Did she care at all for Joe?

She thought for a minute, then said quickly, "No. But he's such a good guy."

The accent was so exactly that of Joe himself that I couldn't help laughing. Her eyes crinkled up and her wide mouth opened to show her fine strong teeth as she threw back her head and laughed too. She had a laugh which rippled up and down—charming—and a contrast to the usual harsh German laugh. Then, suddenly remembering her black clothes and the bereavement, she stopped, saying, "How can I laugh with Pappi still lying unburied?" and rushed off, saying she was late for her work.

It was one of the very darkest afternoons of the whole winter when I called on Frau Altmann. We have many such in London and they never fail to give me the feeling that at any minute the end of the world may come. There was a fog covering half the city.

I was shown into the sitting-room by Frau Luise, Hermann's wife, and found it quite unrecognizable. Black drapes covered the pictures and the doorways. Great wreaths of evergreens were hung with black and purple ribbons, and at the table a group of black-robed women were writing black-edged cards.

Lilli was at a rehearsal, said her mother, after I had been greeted in muted tones. Frau Altmann was paler than usual, but she held her head in its usual high proud poise.

I thought how fine was her profile against the black drapes. In the strange half-light of the room the group of women reminded me of a Rembrandt painting, their sombre clothes melting away into the shadows, and the pale luminosity of their faces and hands giving the scene that sense of drama peculiar to him. I thought of the room as I had so often seen it—with the pink lamp glowing and the family sitting round the stove quarrelling as to who should sit on the wooden box. It was quite alien now.

Frau Altmann drew me to a chair which was strange to me. It was, I found, lent with several others by her sister-in-law. I had time to notice the new lines of grief in her face, the scrupulous neatness of her hair and the immaculate tiny white edge to her high-necked black dress. The girls were both working—jobs were hard to get, and there was always a list of people waiting to step into one's shoes if one stayed away too long. They would both have to ask for time off for the funeral, she said, when they had arranged the date, and here she burst into tears and drew me into the discussion over the grave. She was a woman who believed absolutely in all the teachings of the Church, and I knew that here one must tread very warily so as not to offend or give a wrong impression.

Didn't I think it would be against the teaching of the Church to disturb a soul from his eternal rest by changing his grave? Had I heard what an infamous thing was proposed? They had paid good money for the family plot. How could they have foreseen that one of them would need the grave before the thaw set in? The undertaker and the cemetery authorities seemed to think that people were ghouls and should anticipate such events which were in the hands of God alone.

The other women to whom she introduced me between her tears agreed with her. Their clothes stank of mothballs, and with the smoke from the stove the room was overpowering. Her husband, bless his dear soul, was in the next room. Ursula was now sleeping on the couch in here and Frau Altmann was sharing Lilli's room.

They had managed to get a coffin at last and the funeral would take place as soon as this trouble over the grave was settled. Wouldn't I like to come and look at Oskar? I dared not say that I would rather not. I had learned that it was customary here for all friends to look at the corpse, and I went with her into the bedroom. The peace on the old man's face was quite lovely. He had a dignity far above all this petty bickering going on over the place where his body should rest.

At last came the dreaded question, put directly to me, what were my views about the grave? I stalled. What did the Herr Pastor think? He had been upset too, but he had said that there was nothing to be done except to bury Herr Altmann in one of the graves already dug. What did I myself think? I said firmly that the Pastor was right. She must abide by his decision. What could it matter where the body was buried? The soul, once it had left the body, could not be affected by any such thing.

It seemed to me that this was the time to produce the coffee and cakes which I had brought. The atmosphere was gloomy and lachrymose in the extreme. It was fantastic that this group of black-robed women should be sitting on this winter afternoon solemnly debating whether or not the enforced temporary grave of Herr Altmann could in any way disturb his soul's rest. Only eighteen months ago they had witnessed scenes of bloody violence in the streets and seen their fellow Berliners trampled on by the victorious Red Army and buried in mass graves. Had they already forgotten it? Had they also forgotten that thousands of bodies still lay in the unhallowed ruins here in Berlin? Why, then, all this fuss about the disposal of one? Ursula, with the terrifyingly clear vision of a too rapidly achieved maturity, had seen it in this way, and was impatient, but these women clung, in spite of all the horrors they had undergone, to the conventional—or was it that they thought their only safety lay in the resumption of the conventional pattern of life?

When I said that I had seen Ursula that morning, a fresh trouble was apparent. Frau Altmann's placid control again left her as she gave way to her feelings about her daughter. Ursula was *not* improving. She was painted up like any street girl. She used horrible American slang. She smoked, and was forever swaying about and jiggling her body to the rhythm of the newest dance tunes. She kept horribly late hours, and she told her mother nothing of her doings.

The coffee restored her somewhat and she busied herself serving her guests with the cakes. It was true that the influence of America was very noticeable in the regions where the U.S. troops were stationed, and the transformation of Ursula into a hard-boiled imitation of a Middle West girl was not so surprising. There were thousands of others changing in the same way. She was trying to be the sort of girl Joe would have if he were back home.

I had now resumed teaching again at the British school— the new term had begun, and no teachers had yet arrived from England. They were due at any time now, but the Brigadier in his letter of thanks for my help had asked me to continue a little longer. The A.T.S. took some of my time now too, as their sergeant who taught them cooking had fallen out of a window and broken her arms, and the Major had induced me to take over her cookery classes. They were taking a House-wifery Course; who could be better, he said, than a housewife to teach them?

On the way to school next day, Stampie was very preoccupied. I asked him what was wrong. It was, he explained, the problem of getting Herr Altmann to his grave. No transport of any kind could be found to bear the old man's coffin. The undertaker hadn't a single horse, and there was no petrol for the one hearse available. There was, he said, nothing to be done but for the family to do what other mourners were forced to do if they wanted their dead buried—to take the coffin on a handcart.

The ground was appallingly slippery and I had a vision of Frau Altmann as I had first seen her at the roundabout junction, with the cart running away from her, only this time it would be the coffin falling on to the glassy road.

Stampie looked at me and I looked at him. Neither of us had any need to say what was in our minds. I had already made my apologies to the Altmanns about not being able to attend the funeral. It was at three o'clock and my cooking class was at two.

I had a pretty shrewd idea where Stampie would be while I was teaching those young women to cook.

It began to snow again during the afternoon, and as I watched the huge flakes falling I had a picture in my mind of a little party pushing that handcart. German coffins are made of solid oak and terribly heavy. My husband had told me this after he had twice acted as pall-bearer for British colleagues. I hoped that Stampie would be helping. Hermann wouldn't be much use, and the women were too frail. Stampie was as hard and tough as possible. He often surprised me when he swung John about.

The girls round the large kitchen table were taking down recipes from me. Looking over the shoulder of one I was astonished to see the spelling: "Take ten ounsses of flower, and five ounsses of buter and rub the fat into the flower and need to a dow with a littel water." The girl who was writing this was, she told me, twenty-three, and already had one stripe. Afterwards when checking the recipes in their notebooks I found that the standard of spelling was appallingly low, and none of them except one had ever done any cooking at all. Mum, they said, would not risk the rations. The one who had cooked had been married for a time to a Canadian. She had found that he was a two-timer with a wife and children in Canada. Pity the cooking didn't kill him, she said bluntly.

The snow fell steadily while the cakes baked in the ovens, and the Major paid us a brief but very interested visit. When fifteen cakes of varying quality were turned out safely by the proud cooks, there was Stampie waiting for me, looking like Father Christmas. The car was covered in snow, and he was shaking it out of his greatcoat as a retriever dog does.

"Like Siberia up at that cemetery," he observed, brushing vigorously at his cap while the snowflakes fell on his well-oiled hair. "Never was in a more desolate place in my life."

"Is poor old Herr Altmann safely buried at last?" I asked.

He nodded. "We didn't need any loose earth—the snow covered him." Then he added thoughtfully, "Funny thing. This old car always did remind me of a hearse."

If I had made any comment he would probably have told me that although we were forbidden to carry live Germans in our cars, there was no regulation that he knew of against carrying dead ones. He was an old soldier and knew the regulations on every point.

I remarked that it must have been a bit bumpy as the springs were none too good.

"Less bumpy than a handcart with several spills on the way," he chuckled. "Although, for that matter ..." A grin passed over his face and he stopped.

"What if you'd been challenged by the Military Police?" I said, for we were often stopped and checked by them.

"I covered the coffin with that rug of yours. He was small—and if they'd asked—well, I was delivering your wreath. It was there on top of the rug."

I wondered that this man who had gone through such a lot in the war should have been willing to take such a risk for a dead German.

"He reminded me of my old Dad," he said, as if answering my unspoken question; "a nice gentle old boy—wouldn't have hurt a fly. Shouldn't have liked my old Dad to have gone to his grave on a handcart. You'd better tuck that rug round you, M'm, it'll keep you warmer than it did him. It's perishing today."

We stopped to give a lift to some friends of mine, and I had to wait until the evening for the whole story.

The coffin had been so heavy and the ground so slippery that progress had been agonizingly painful. The undertaker and his men had helped him load it into the car, but he dared not take them with him, or any member of the family. The Military Police were always on the look-out to see that we did not give lifts to Germans. The widow and the two girls set off by the U-bahn with Hermann and the mourners.

The car had skidded badly once and the coffin slid heavily against one door, the lock of which was broken. The door opened—and for one awful moment Stampie thought that Herr Altmann had gone. He stopped the car just in time to save the coffin from falling into the road. It was perilously balanced, but he was not strong enough to push it back on to the floor of the car at the only angle at which it would fit in. He stood there heaving at it with his whole strength to no avail.

Fortunately for him the weather was so awful that there was no one about on the road, add the thickly falling snow hindered visibility. A solitary passer-by refused suspiciously to help heave until Stampie had produced a whole packet of cigarettes. The man then willingly lent his shoulders and between them they finally got Herr Altmann back into the car. No questions were asked by the stranger, nor was any explanation offered by Stampie. The man took the cigarettes, asked for matches, and disappeared happily into the snow.

After that Stampie drove very cautiously until he reached the cemetery. It was a bleak bare place and, as he said, could have been anywhere in Siberia on that afternoon. The light was already failing, and the little which remained was worsened by the snowstorm which never let up for one moment.

It was a very long time before the mourners arrived. They had had a long walk after the U-bahn journey, but the Pastor was already there and half frozen. He accepted a cigarette and a seat in the car most gratefully.

Stampie had driven the car right into the cemetery as near to the grave as he could get. The grave-diggers looked like frozen gnomes huddled against the wall with sacks over their heads and shoulders. They were longing to get away and find some shelter from the snow. So hard was the frost that they had been obliged to use their pickaxes to break up the mound of what had been loose earth for filling in the graves.

It was almost dark when the funeral party arrived, and it took all the men—the Pastor included—all their strength to shoulder the coffin and bear it to the grave. If one man did not slip, another did, and they were constantly swaying and sliding, with Herr Altmann performing a macabre dance of death on their shoulders.

There should have been a wheeled bier on which to place the coffin, but like everything else it had disappeared—probably stolen for the wood or wheels, said the Pastor. Thieves had no qualms nowadays, and even hacked up the pews and the wooden collection boxes for firewood.

Ursula had been ordered to wipe the lipstick from her mouth, and remove her nail-varnish before leaving the house. Frau Altmann had been dissatisfied with her appearance. She was, said her mother, too vulgarly conspicuous to attend something which should have been sacred to her.

Ursula had been furious. The lipstick would not come off easily; it was, she said, permanent. She had removed the bright red nail-varnish reluctantly, saying that her father could not see it, and that, under her gloves, neither could the mourners.

Frau Altmann and her daughters had stood by the coffin with the Pastor, Hermann, Luise, Stampie and a few friends. Stampie said that they were all three veiled with thin black veils and that the girls looked quite lovely. Lilli, he said, had an almost unearthly beauty in the cold failing light, her small triangular face and shining hair showing through the veil. Ursula, on the contrary, looked quite terribly alive and vital among these others, ageing and resigned. She looked, he said, as if she had so many lovely things to do that she was unwilling to waste any time on the dead.

The snow got thicker and thicker, and the Pastor's voice quicker and quicker as he strove to finish his sad task before they were all frozen. His teeth were chattering, but his voice was steady as he read the solemn service which is almost exactly the same as our own.

Frau Altmann wept as she was handed the scoop of earth, and with it scattered some flowers into the grave after the perilous task of lowering the coffin had been achieved. None of the men with the exception of Stampie had the strength for such a task. Their diet was simply not sufficient for any form of heavy manual labour. It had been quite horrible, and Hermann, whose strength had been sapped by alcohol as well as lack of food, had collapsed suddenly, and for a moment or two they thought that he had gone to join his brother. Stampie had scandalized the mourners by giving him a swig of schnapps from his pocket flask. He hadn't any brandy, but the Steinhager had done just as well. The Pastor had continued steadily with the service while Hermann revived sufficiently to stand up for the last amen.

Stampie was a born story-teller. He made this scene so real for me, illustrating his points with his own inimitable gestures and remarks, that I asked him to take me to see the grave which had now been filled in roughly and covered with a few frozen wreaths and flowers. It had stopped snowing and the sky was slate-grey with the bulging look of more to come. I never saw a more desolate cemetery anywhere in the world. There wasn't a bush or tree to be seen—all had been ruthlessly hewn down for fuel—just a vast expanse of snow, out of which the headstones and crosses rose like ghostly sentinels.

X V

I KEPT MY promise to Frau Altmann and tried to get news of Fritz, although Stampie was positive that by now he had fled into the Russian Zone. I had seen her several times since her husband's death and found her calm but terribly unhappy. She said very little, but I sensed the almost numbed grief in which the double shock of Oskar's death and Fritz's flight had submerged her. She asked me to give her more work to do for the babies—she found relief in doing things, she said. It seemed to me that there were many things waiting to be done for Lilli, but she appeared completely blind to the needs of her daughters. She asked me again and again to try and get news of Fritz. I don't know how she thought I could do so, but she had a fixed belief that I would find him.

I discovered from Ursula the names of all the places he had frequented for his Black Market deals, and one evening when my husband was at a late conference Stampie and I did the round of the night clubs and cafes.

First we went to Sophie's, for she had been friendly with Fritz and had done quite a bit of business with the brother and sister. Her place was quite new, and had sprung up as so many others had done, like a mushroom overnight. Hers could have been any night club in any capital in the world, except that it was much better furnished and appointed than most. Thick carpets and heavy curtains shut out the cold, the table linen was immaculate, the silver good, and there were flowers and discreet lighting. The orchestra was playing *Liebling mit dem blonden Haar* as we entered. It was terribly hot in there as one came in from the icy wind outside. Sophie knew Stampie quite well, and we were warmly greeted, but she had seen nothing of Fritz.

We drank some wine with her and she saw us off solicitously. She wanted a pair of shoes—couldn't I get them for her? She'd give me anything, pay *anything* for them. Everyone wanted something, from elastic to keep up their underclothes to pins, needles and buttons, and every kind of tablet and medicament. Sometimes I told Lotte that if anyone asked me for one more thing I should scream.

We went on to Bobby's Bar, to Johnnie's Bar and then to the café on the Reichskanzlerecke. This was the place I liked—it was always full of the most fascinating people, and I longed for my sketchbook. No one knew anything at all about Fritz. Ursula had already been there inquiring for her brother and had settled the account he had run up for drinks.

There was still time to spare and I asked to see some of the night clubs in the U.S. sector. In one place painted to represent a blue lagoon there were astonishing frescoes of well-fed nude girls dancing under a tropical sun. They were good, and I asked about the artist who had painted them. He was dead, said the proprietor carelessly—did I think the paintings any good? I asked of what he had died and if he were young. He had been very young and he had killed himself, said the man with a shrug of his shoulders. He had fed the lad for a month in return for his frescoes, but he couldn't do it any longer. No one wanted works of art now—they wanted food, food, *food!* It was of far more value than money.

The blue water in the lagoon had some kind of mechanical device behind it causing it to move in a rise and swell—I could imagine that after a few drinks one could feel sea-sick just from looking at it. The music was slow, dreamy and voluptuous. The couples on the floor were so tightly locked together that all they could indulge in was necking.

"Come on! We can't stay in here—Christ, it makes me sick!" Stampie pulled me firmly through the door into the fresh air. We went to two more, much the same, but with no news of Fritz. If any of them knew anything, which was doubtful, they were not telling.

Stampie suggested a snack at the American snack-bar in Kronprinzenallee.

"We have to pay in dollar scrip," I objected.

"Got plenty," he said grinning. "I like to bring Johnnie here and watch him eating ice cream sundaes."

We ate hot dogs and fried eggs between rounds of thickly buttered bread—then chocolate ice cream with marshmallow sauce. It was wonderful after our monotonous army rations, with its bully beef and egg powder which tasted of fish. The only shell eggs we had seen since our arrival had been two which Frau von R.'s hens had laid and which she had insisted on giving to John.

The German waitresses behind the bar wore chintz frocks and tiny frilled aprons with large provocative bows on their heads. They said, "You're welcome!" when we thanked them. Their accents ranged from New England to California, and it was difficult to believe that until a year ago most of them had never spoken a word of English.

On the way back we looked in again at the café on the Reichskanzlerecke, as we thought Joe and Ursula might be there. They were not, and we came away quickly. A fracas was going on between three coloured sergeants and two huge G.I.'s. They had been fighting, but suddenly finished quite amicably, for they all scrambled up from the débris of the broken table and crockery, shook hands all round, and produced wads of notes to pay for the damage they had done. A minute later, as we left, U.S. Military Police cars came screaming round the corner, but the brawlers had all been let out of a side door by that time.

"Well! We're certainly seeing life, although we haven't found Fritz," said Stampie as we went home.

It was just after the most magnificent Red Army Day party at which General Sokolovsky had entertained us in the lovely Sans Souci Palace at Potsdam—now the Russian headquarters—that I encountered my first returning prisoner from Russia.

I was with Peggy, a very charming new neighbour, whose little sons played with John. We had been seeing some friends off at Charlottenburg station and as we were coming away she clutched my arm, saying "My God! Just look at that!"

A young man, as emaciated as a scarecrow, in rags, and walking with agonizing difficulty, was hobbling in the same direction as we were. It wasn't the sores on his hands or the bare bleeding feet bound to pieces of wood in place of shoes which made one catch one's breath—but the look on his young face.

We stopped and offered him a lift. He got in after some hesitation, and sat next to the German driver whose contempt and aversion for this poor derelict were apparent as he drew himself away.

We questioned the boy. He had just come from Russia and had found his family gone and his home in ruins. He had been captured in Stalingrad in '43. Where was he going now? He didn't know, but he thought that his aunt in Westphalia might still be alive. He had to find the fare and obtain the permit to leave Berlin and go into the British Zone. We drove back to the Grunewald, and as Peggy's flat was on the ground floor took him in there. The maid who opened the door to us exclaimed in horror and disgust at the gnädige Frau bringing in such people. Peggy turned on her like a tigress.

"When I see people like you and the driver behaving in this way, then I understand Belsen, Buchenwald and all those other places," she said fiercely. "This man is one of *you*! He's a German. He fought for *you*! And this is how you receive him when he comes home after years in a prison camp!"

The woman merely remarked that the gnädige Frau had better be careful, there were lice and other unpleasant things in prison camps. She was eyeing the rags with horror and disgust.

"Fetch the cook," ordered her mistress. This woman was equally shocked, but anxious to help, as Peggy told her to get a meal ready and to bring coffee immediately. The boy did not want to sit in a chair—he said it was years since he had sat on anything except the bare floor—he was too dirty for a chair, he apologized.

"Would you like a hot bath?" asked Peggy.

He was incredulous, saying that a bath was something of which they had dreamed for years in the prison camps. While the disgusted maid went to prepare a bath he talked to us. He had come from Sverdlovsk in the Urals, he said. There were a great many prison camps round Sverdlovsk, as the Russians were building enormously round this, the capital of the Urals. They employed the prisoners, working in bitter cold, on digging out the foundations for building railways and new roads. Why had he been released? He was ill—he had already had several haemorrhages of the lungs. The Russians had sent him to Sevro, almost at the North Pole, he told us. It was a wonderful health centre for that part of Russia, and was full of tubercular patients. The doctors had been kind and he had received treatment for his lungs, but the cold had been appalling. Thousands of prisoners died from the cold in Sverdlovsk—they had been frozen to death. In Sevro the food was better than in Sverdlovsk, where they had been kept ravenously hungry. After a year in Sevro they had told him that he would be released. He could do no more work.

We asked if there were many civilian prisoners. Thousands, he said, and women as well as men. The women had mostly been kidnapped from the East Zone of Germany and transported to Russian labour camps. They were fairly well treated—the Russians were not cruel, and they hadn't much food themselves. I asked him if he had seen the terrible destruction which Germany had vented on Russian towns and villages. He had both seen it and been told of it—again and again—the Russians saw to that, he said.

We asked what the Russian people in the far north were like? They were, he said, so fit and physically perfect that in the Urals they could walk barefooted in the snow without frostbite. They had beautiful teeth and fine strong bodies, could endure great hardships and had a fanatical love of their country. They were a marvellous race; although they had few luxuries they were happy and would sing and dance in the evenings after work. Did they grumble? Of course—quite a lot. Did he speak Russian? Yes, all prisoners were taught Russian as soon as they arrived. At the end of five years' labour the civilian prisoners could do as they pleased—return to their homeland or stay in Russia—and some chose to stay.

We were astonished to hear this. Peggy and I could have listened to him all day, but he was tired, and we searched for some clothes for him to put on after his bath.

He was pathetically grateful, and after the bath, in clean clothes, having enjoyed a good meal and a cigarette, he looked quite different but alarmingly ill. He had cleaned the bath most carefully, Peggy told me, not having missed the expression on the maid's face. When he tried to thank us he broke down and cried like a child. He wasn't much more—having been sent to the Eastern front at sixteen and a half.

We took him to the Social Welfare Centre where I knew the officials. They were always willing to help and promised to arrange the permits for him to go to Westphalia.

I thought that perhaps Frau Altmann would like to talk with him. Her son Kurt had been captured at Stalingrad too, and she had not received a word from him since then. This boy told us that he had never received any news from his home, although he knew that his parents would have written, so that it was quite likely that Kurt Altmann was alive. Now that he looked so different it would not be so painful for Frau Altmann to see him. She had heard through another returned prisoner that Kurt had been in Sverdlovsk at one time, and I hoped that it might buoy up her hopes of Kurt coming home again to see and talk to this lad.

She went to the Social Welfare Centre and saw him. She took him all kinds of little things, Ursula told me, and talked with him for hours. She saw him off at the station on his way to Westphalia and told me that he bore absolutely no animosity towards the Russians—indeed he liked the peasant people.

Later we got a letter from him, and one from his mother, whom he had found safely at his aunt's home near Herford. A postcript to the mother's letter of thanks told us that her son's lungs were beyond repair—nothing could be done for him.

"Supposing it had been one of our sons," said Peggy when we had read this. "Wouldn't we have blessed any woman who did for ours the little that we did for him?"

I told her about Fritz, of whom there was still no news, and whom we thought must certainly be in the Russian Zone. Many lads were being lured there with the promise of a uniform, a job and good pay. Being allowed to march again to a band, even if the flag under which they marched was a hammer and sickle in place of a swastika, meant a great deal to a German.

Swastikas were definitely out. All Nazi literature and flags had been burned by order of the Allies, and it was a punishable offence to possess either.

"But you can't burn memories," sighed Frau Altmann, "and the young people have not forgotten that evil régime— to them it was thrilling, exciting and glorious to march with those jack-booted monsters."

Sometimes we would see a swastika chalked up on a wall or pavement. The Germans had no flags, no uniforms and no bands now. They were all forbidden. The Russians promised them all three, and they could march to *The Red Flag* or to the rousing tune of *Brüder zur Sonne zur Freiheit* if they wished. Some excellent propaganda films were already helping this project.

XVI

IT WAS AT a special matinee of the ballet that Lilli collapsed on the stage, and I realised that she was really ill. She had been quite excited about this matinée, for she was an ambitious dancer and practised assiduously by herself. They were going to dance Debussy's *L'Après-midi d'un Faune*. I did not expect too much, for their ballet standard did not come up to ours, but Lilli had told me that the boy who was going to dance the Faun was wonderful—he could leap almost as high as Nijinsky had done when he had created the famous rôle.

Lilli herself was still in the corps de ballet, but that she would soon reach individual rôles was obvious if only her health stood the strain. I had learned about the essential points necessary in a ballerina from a former famous one and was convinced that Lilli had all that was needed, plus ambition and infinite patience. Here in Berlin she stood little chance, for ballet was merely a subsidiary part of the opera. I had told her about the Sadlers Wells Ballet which would soon be coming to Germany, and had planned to take her to see them.

I went alone to the matinée. The *Faune* came first, and it was the first time I had seen it danced. The orchestra seemed unfamiliar with Debussy's music. They had probably not been allowed to play it under the rigid Nazi regime, but Lilli was right about the boy—he was promising.

A new Spanish ballet followed this, and it was then that I saw Lilli stumble, recover herself, then collapse in a heap. Her partner's quickness and cleverness in picking her up and bearing her off as if in the abandonment of the dance prevented anyone from realising that she had actually collapsed. She did not reappear, and after the ballet ended I went round backstage to inquire for her. She had just come out of a long faint, and the group of dancers around were concerned, wanting to fetch a doctor, but Lilli was protesting vehemently that she was all right, that by the time the doctor arrived she would be safely at home. Doctors had no cars, or petrol, and were lucky if the Russians had left them a bicycle for their rounds.

She looked so ill that I was alarmed too, and begged her to let me take her to one of my several women doctor friends. She protested quite hysterically, saying that if I could possibly give her a lift home she would be perfectly all right. Her friend Susi was looking after her and promised to help her to dress, for she was still in the Spanish costume which had so enchanted her.

The stage manager told me that his girls were constantly fainting now. It was hard for them, but life was hard for everyone these days and they must be thankful to get their weekly salary still, when so many actresses were out of work. The opera was playing to packed houses every night—the Allies being a most appreciative audience.

Lilli was dressed by this time, and I took her home with me. She accepted a cup of tea but would not eat anything. She sat very still and quiet in a chair just as she had done on her previous visit when she had come to pose for me and I had seen that she was too exhausted. She watched John playing with the puppies. He was throwing a ball across the room and the two ridiculous creatures raced madly to get it, each trying to push the other away. It was Whiskey who invariably got the ball—he was much bigger and stronger than Soda.

"The male always gets the best of it," she observed sadly.

I thought that in Germany it had certainly always been so, but now things were changing.

"Mutti is always looking at every youth she sees, hoping that it will be Fritz," she said. "He still means far more to her than Ursi and I do, in spite of all he has done."

John, who had hurt himself, came running to me for comfort and I took him on my lap and cuddled him. She looked at us with a strange expression in her lovely eyes. They were so dark a violet blue today that they seemed almost black. When I put him down I saw that two tears were running slowly down her cheeks. I knew that something more than the faint was troubling her but did not like to question her, for it was evident that she was in no state to answer.

She said, with a long weary sigh, "How lovely it is to be in a nice chair—I am so very tired."

She lay there utterly exhausted. Her pallor was alarming. I gave her a pair of ballet shoes which had come from Brussels. When I found that the first pair had fitted so well I had ordered a second pair through some Belgian friends there. She was delighted—quite speechless with pleasure as she fingered them. They were to her the tools of her trade, as were my brushes, paints and canvas to me. German artists had none of these things now.

She had confided to me that she longed more than anything else to dance the rôle of Giselle. It is the most exacting of rôles, requiring not only great technical skill but considerable acting ability as well as plain staying power. I told her it was one of my favourite ballets, and one which we do not perform very often in England.

At the house Frau Altmann plied me with questions about the matinee. She had declined my invitation to accompany me, having been quite shocked at the idea of attending a theatre so soon after her husband's death. She had made me feel that I was ignorant of social etiquette to have even suggested such a thing. In spite of the convulsions and ravages of war there were apparently still rigid rules about etiquette.

Lilli had insisted that we did not tell her mother she had fainted. She was looking a little better now. I had slipped some brandy in her tea. Frau Altmann, however, was too wrapped up in her own grief to have noticed. I thought that she ought to be told—that it would be a good thing to shake her from her apathy by pointing out the growing fragility of this little daughter of hers, to force her to realise that if something was not done about Lilli's health she would soon be following her father to the grave.

I did not do it. Lilli had begged me not to, and it was, after all, none of my business. Frau Altmann might have resented it very much. But I did mention it to Stampie who was himself worried about Lilli. He was, I knew, meeting Ursula and her friend Joe that evening and he promised to speak to her.

Ursula, however, had disgusted him when she had arrived with Joe at Sophie's that night. They were both more than half seas over, said Stampie, and their flagrant necking in public had embarrassed Stampie, who, although anything but a prude, had, as he pointed out to me, definite standards.

Lilli, Ursula had insisted, was perfectly all right. She had always looked like a dying angel from childhood and everyone had petted and made a fuss of her because of this look. Lilli got the best out of life, and gave precious little herself. She was, in her sister's opinion, rather a fraud. That pale complexion and paler hair giving her the air of being, as the Americans said, "out of this world." She was in fact, said her sister spitefully, no saint although their mother thought her one, and their father had always doted on her.

Stampie came away with the impression that Ursula was at heart rather jealous of her younger sister, and under the influence of Joe's drinks had rather let her tongue run away with her. She was normally a good-natured girl, generous to a fault.

I could understand Ursula's feelings. She had been obliged to give up her musical training to keep the home going. While she was doing household chores and ruining her hands Lilli had been able to continue in her profession because the opera was in such demand that dancers could still earn a living.

Jealousy and envy were, I was finding, characteristic traits in many Germans. To get someone into trouble was a feather in one's cap. Children were encouraged to report each other, and were rewarded for it. Lotte had told me about this, as had Dr Annemarie. It was not merely a Nazi innovation to encourage children to spy on each other and their neighbours.

The petty jealousies and spite among the German staffs of many British homes astonished us, and the ensuing trouble was apt to make one overlook the many good qualities in them— their punctuality, their diligence, their honesty and their complete devotion to the family for whom they were working. British children were being left in the care of German women for weeks while their parents were away in the Zone, and I never heard of one case in which the German failed in her duty and care of the children.

If Stampie was disgusted that Ursula was drinking too much and getting hard-boiled, her mother was far more so. Yet from where did Frau Altmann think that the money for the daily necessities of life was coming? With prices still at a fantastic level, the simplest standard of life cost a fortune.

Ursula had conceived the very sensible idea of making a pair of slacks for herself out of some old trousers of her father's. Every woman in Berlin seemed to have been wearing her husband's trousers this winter for warmth, and Ursula and Lilli both needed some. Frau Altmann was genuinely horrified at the idea. The trousers were to be kept for Kurt and Fritz. Both would surely return one day and would need them. She had never dreamed that a daughter of hers could ever want to be seen in men's trousers. It was shameful and disgusting. She hated the slacks which German women had worn during the war, and this idea of wearing her husband's trousers was revolting to her.

A few days later, Ursula appeared in a pair of well-cut slacks, and when questioned said bluntly that they had been given her by a man.

Frau Altmann was bitter about this when I met her at a friend's house one afternoon. She had been giving a German lesson to three British wives. What did I think of the trousers? Wasn't it disgusting?

I said I thought it was a matter of necessity for many. They hadn't got any warm clothes left, and to see the missing husbands' warm trousers hanging in the cupboards waiting for the moths was too much.

She said flatly, "But you British ladies don't wear them."

We did, but it wasn't worth while explaining to her that having lived in them during the war we were glad to get out of them.

I asked how the lessons were going. Very well indeed. Had the ladies expressed themselves as satisfied with her teaching? I assured her that they were very pleased, and that there were several children wanting a small class formed for German— would she care to take them on? She would. It was better to be busy. One didn't think so much.

She was, I thought, less passive than when I had first met her, her face having less acceptance of fate in it. She was beginning to wake up to some new facts which she was having to learn in a very hard school.

XVII

HAD MY MIND not been taken up with John during the next fortnight, the story of Lilli might have been different, for I was determined to do something about her. She lay on my conscience—perhaps because I felt such an affinity with her. She was driven by some force to dance just as I was to paint, and tired or not she went on striving. Her frailty touched some chord every time I saw her—just as her dancing moved me emotionally. I had decided to have her to lunch when John was at school and to ask her to let me send her to a sanatorium in the Black Forest about which I had been told.

Just as I was planning this, however, John fell while playing shipwreck with his little friends. He only fell off our own table and the cut he sustained on his head was very slight. Knowing that cuts and abrasions did not heal in Berlin now, because of either the infected dust of the ruins or our poor diet, I took him at once to our M.O., who assured me that it was nothing. But the next day he was ill, with a temperature which rose rapidly while his head began to swell. It is unnecessary to go into all the trouble we had with the M.O., whose negligence almost cost John his life, but the outcome was that we had to rush the child to the Spandau Military Hospital where a very clever and attentive young lieutenant in the R.A.M.C. told us that we had only just brought him in time, and began pumping penicillin into John, who was unconscious with a temperature of nearly 105.

He saved John's life—or as he said, the penicillin did. We were forbidden to consult German doctors and dentists, and although both Dr Gaupp and Dr Annemarie had offered to get him into their children's hospital, I could not accept. We lived under Military orders and were reminded of it frequently. These two were quite wonderful in their constant inquiries, advice, and offers of help, as were many Germans at this terrible time. A letter brought to me from Frau Altmann told me that she was positive that John would recover—that she was praying for him—that God would not let my child die, because of all the little ones I was helping to save. All the Germans told me this. It seemed extraordinary to me that they could believe this after seeing so many innocent children die every day now. But they did believe it, and were overjoyed when I was able to tell them that he was off the danger list and would soon be home again.

Stampie, who had shared our terrible anxiety and who had taken us on that nightmare journey to Spandau in a snowstorm with John wrapped up in blankets, unconscious in his father's arms, was quite overcome at the news. There were tears in his eyes as he said, "I don't mind telling you I went on a blind last night—I was that upset about the little chap—if anything had happened to him I'd have shot that M.O."

During John's convalescence I was kept busy trying to amuse and divert him, for the huge amount of penicillin had a depressing effect on him, and this combined with my classes at the Study Centre took all my time. Ursula came in and out with notes and messages from her mother, who found all kinds of tiny things to amuse the patient. Ursula said that she had found them all tucked away in a box of toys in their cellar.

The mother of the little Scottish boys, who was now a friend of mine and who came frequently to inquire for John, told me that she was worried about her little housemaid. The girl had gone to a certain address for what was ostensibly a small operation, but as she had refused all offers to get her into an accredited hospital my friend Sally feared that she might be going to undergo an abortion. She asked me if I would go and have a look at the place for her. She asked me because I spoke German and she did not. Stampie, who was at a loose end, having some unwanted leave, offered to go for me. It would be easier for him, he explained; he knew so many people in that area. Sally's fears were well grounded. It was exactly the kind of place which she had expected it to be. It was run, apparently, by a sister of Sophie's, who, as Stampie said grimly, probably supplied most of the clients—but that was not all. He had seen Lilli going in there. I said that he must have been mistaken. It was impossible. He insisted that it *was* Lilli—he would know her anywhere—few girls had either her very fair hair worn in a knot or her very slender build. She had been wearing her black coat and the little astrakhan cap—and was hurrying so much that she hadn't noticed him.

"She must have been visiting a friend there," I said, although it didn't seem likely.

Ursula had said that Lilli was tired, but otherwise quite well when I had asked after her. They had been having a very heavy season, and Lilli was coming home later and later every night, said Ursula. I sent her some small luxuries with a note saying that I would come to fetch her for lunch as soon as John was off my hands, and I did not think any more of what Stampie had told me.

It was no longer quite so cold, every day the sun came out quite strongly. There was a sparkle and exhilaration in the air which were like wine. We went skating at our Blue and White Club and at the Study Centre where they had flooded the tennis courts.

Returning one afternoon from skating I found Ursula waiting for me. I had not seen her for a week owing to having been so occupied. She looked tired today, with shadows under her eyes, and told me at once that Lilli was very ill. They were trying to get her into hospital—could I please help? They thought it was an appendicitis which had turned to peritonitis, but they didn't really know. I questioned her further, as she seemed so embarrassed and upset, and finally she blurted out that her sister was having an abortion.

At once I remembered what Stampie had told me about having seen Lilli going into that infamous house run by Sophie's sister.

Ursula said that Lilli had been very quiet for some time now, but that as she was secretive by nature it had been useless to ask her what was wrong. Ursula had been positive that there was a man in Lilli's life. Now she was really very ill—in a high fever and in terrible pain. I asked how long she had been ill. Only two days, said Ursula. Lilli had come home from the

Opera House looking ghastly one night, had admitted that she was ill, and had gone at once to bed.

The two girls shared a room, and it was impossible for Lilli to hide from her sister what was happening to her. In the morning she could not get out of bed and was in a high fever.

Ursula had gone for their family doctor—the one who had done what he could for Herr Altmann. He had said that hospital was imperative at once. Ursula had come straight to me.

Frau Altmann did not seem to have taken in the cause of Lilli's illness. She had concluded that it was a ruptured appendix, but the doctor had informed her bluntly that there had been a deliberate abortion, and that it would probably be a police matter if they could find out who was responsible for it.

Ursula said that she had thought her mother would strike the doctor in her indignation and shock. She simply would not believe him. He seemed astounded that she knew nothing of her daughter's state of health, saying that Lilli was extremely ill, quite apart from the abortion—he thought that she definitely had tuberculosis and that both lungs were affected.

"Mutti has been so wrapped up in her grief for Pappi and Fritz that she simply had no eyes for Lilli or me," said Ursula bitterly.

I thought that no one had had time for Lilli, who must have been ill for a long time and who had never been robust. As to the other trouble, said Ursula, who would have imagined such a thing of the immaculate Lilli? There was, I observed, a certain satisfaction mixed with Ursula's grief. The "good" little sister, who had always been held up to her as an example, was now in a shameful plight. I telephoned to the head doctor at a big women's hospital which I was helping with linen and bandages. He promised a bed for Lilli, and also to get in touch with her doctor at once.

I asked Ursula if she had walked to me, and suggested that I came back with her and saw Lilli. She hesitated, and then said that Lilli had asked her to get me, but that Frau Altmann hadn't liked it—and burst into tears. Stampie was away on leave, but I got a taxi from our British service and went with her to the house.

Frau Altmann greeted me with a face of stone. The doctor was with Lilli, she said. I went in, and he looked at the things I had brought with approval. He needed just those, he said; was I able to help him a little? He had been unable to get a nurse. I told him I had nursed during the war—and in a gynaecological ward part of the time. I could do as I was instructed. The hospital was sending an ambulance for Lilli in the afternoon, but she needed immediate attention.

On the third day that she was in hospital I went to see her. She had asked her mother to beg me to come.

She lay flat in the bed looking as if the wings of death were already hovering over her. Great shadows under her eyes, her small face shrunken and of a bluish pallor. The delicate tapering hands busy with the bedclothes showed me how ill she was.

She had refused to answer any of the doctors' questions and she was too far gone to be bothered by them.

I laid some snowdrops on her pillow. They were just appearing in the shops and could be bought for the eternal cigarettes. She smiled a little, murmuring that it was good of me to come—there was something she wanted to ask me to do for her; but although I stayed some time by her bed, she kept on drowsing off into unconsciousness, murmuring occasionally in her sleep, and she did not tell me what it was she wanted. The head doctor came in and I asked him if there was any chance for her. He shook his head.

"It was too late for the penicillin," he said sadly.

I had managed to get some from an American friend and they had tried it in vain.

I told the sister, whom I knew quite well, that I would come back again in the morning, but Lilli died that evening.

Ursula and her mother were with her when she died, but she told them nothing at all. Frau Altmann had brought the old pastor who had known Lilli from childhood, and he had said that she was not to be worried and had simply said a prayer for her. She had just said that she was so very very tired, and how nice it was to be in hospital. The last word on her lips was "Vova." Just nonsense of delirium, said her mother, who thought that she was imagining herself to be back on the stage. Frau Altmann had prayed steadily until the end, said Ursula.

"Vova" was the same word which she had murmured over and over again in her sleep when I was with her. I had once had a very dear Russian friend who liked to be called Vova, which was the shortened or pet form of his name, Vladimir.

XVIII

LILLI'S DEATH was a terrible blow which shook the ground from under Frau Altmann's feet. Not only her death, but the causes which had accelerated that death. That she could have been so blind to her child's state of mind and health did not astonish me at all. German women are brought up to worship the male members of the family. All her concern had been for Fritz, the missing Kurt, and her husband, despite the fact that her daughters had taken over the job of breadwinners for the family.

She had not noticed the fatigue on the girls' faces when they came home from a long day's work on insufficient food, and she had taken it for granted that they would automatically wait on their father and brother. British and American films were already influencing the German women about the position of the woman in the home. Frau Altmann deplored this. It was unnatural, she thought, to see a man helping in the house. His place was in the office, or sitting by the fire with pipe and slippers. But she listened with interest to my views on the subject—one of her nicest qualities was her willingness to admit that her opinions were not always right. She was the most honest person I have ever met. The fact that it was now far easier for women than for men to obtain employment and earn money spoke for itself. She was beginning to see that it was causing a revolution in many homes.

I collected all the drawings I had made of Lilli and took them to her. There were only two which I kept; one was a sketch of her resting in a chair; this I made on the day when she had been too tired to pose for me—the other was a drawing of her poised on her toes in her balled dress. I liked this one—it had caught something of the extraordinary fragility and the quality of lightness which Lilli had always shown. Among the heavily built German women she had looked as if she had been accidentally blown in by the wind.

Stampie had been away on a few days' leave, and knew nothing of Lilli's illness. He returned the day after her death. The news was a terrible shock to him. He was, in fact, completely bowled over when I told him, and broke down in his grief.

I had had no idea that he was so fond of Lilli. It was Ursula whom he had at first admired and lately grumbled over so much. He had, it seemed, adored Lilli always, but never told her so. In his queer off-hand way he had been devoted to her, and many of the kindnesses he had done this family had been done for Lilli's sake more than Hermann's. Unknown to me, he had gone again and again to the opera just to see her dance in the corps de ballet, and before she had acquired a "friend" he had frequently escorted her home afterwards.

She was, he told me, very like his daughter had been before she had got "snooty" and above her station. What exactly he meant by that, I don't know—both his children had been born before he was twenty-two—he was only forty or so now. His feelings for Lilli, however, had clearly not been entirely fatherly, even if she had reminded him of his daughter Margaret.

I did my best to console him, but he was inconsolable—more so when he learned what had accelerated her death. He said bitterly: "I knew it was Lilli I saw that afternoon. Poor kid, why didn't she tell *us* if she dared not tell her mother?"

I could think of many reasons why she could not tell me—although I think she tried on several occasions. For instance, that conversation about nationality—had it been in her mind then? She had wanted me to do something for her just before she died, but it was too late then. She could not break through the barriers of her innate reticence about herself, and knowing Stampie's feelings for her—for a woman always knows when a man loves her—she could not tell him either.

That evening he and I went to the Staatsoper and went round to see her friend Susi. They were all terribly upset—but not communicative. Susi obviously knew a good deal, but she was not telling. Did she know whose child it had been? If so she never told. Frau Altmann was positive that Lilli had been raped by one of the Russians who frequented the theatre. She would not contemplate any other explanation. Susi told me that Lilli had been terribly in love with someone, but she refused to say any more.

Stampie said that one evening he had seen her with a tall Russian officer—they were dining at the new restaurant which the Russians frequented in their sector. Her usually placid immobility had been transfigured, he said, as if a light was burning inside.

"I knew that he was the one," he said sadly, "because, you see, when you love a person you get a sort of second sight; and when I saw those two together I knew that there was no place for me in her heart."

What was he like? Very good looking, very dark. He could have been a Celt with his blue eyes, said Stampie. He was a very smart immaculate officer, and he and Lilli had been so engrossed in each other that they hadn't even seen Stampie.

That was all we ever knew about Lilli's love affair. She had been so secretive about it that it had cost her her life.

It was only six weeks since Herr Altmann's death but the ground was no longer so hard. There had been rain, and the snow was no longer so frozen, although it still hung about. There were days now when one felt that the wind would surely soon be bringing us a faint scent of spring.

They buried Lilli with her father in the family plot. They had managed to dig the double grave, and Herr Altmann's coffin had been brought from its temporary resting-place.

A great many friends from the Opera House and many former school friends attended Lilli's funeral, and in spite of the dearth of flowers there were innumerable wreaths and flowers.

As Lilli had died in the hospital, the transport to the cemetery was all arranged with far less bother this time than there had been over poor Herr Altmann's funeral cortège.

One was constantly astonished at the German love of giving and receiving small gifts. It is one of their more endearing traits. Gifts are always beautifully tied, and usually decorated with a spray of greenery or a flower; but at funerals they show an over-indulgence in the macabre which contrasts with their usually artistic flower arrangements. The wreaths for the ethereal and light-footed Lilli were mostly of huge heavy evergreens tied with hideous black and purple ribbons and deep black bands. Among them stood out the simple flowers which Stampie and I had sent, and a great sheaf of lilies-of-the-valley. They had come, said Frau Altmann, that morning, from the most expensive flower shop in the Russian sector near the theatre.

There was no black-edged card attached, but the sheaf was tied with a silver ribbon with the word "Lilli" on it. The flowers had been addressed to "Fräulein Lilli Altmann," just as if she were alive, not dead. Her mother had been shocked at this, but the lilies were so lovely that she had put them on the coffin, and they were buried with her.

They must, said Ursula, have cost a fortune, and she had gone herself to the shop from which they had come, to try and find out who had sent them. They had been ordered by telephone, and the money sent round by a child messenger in a sealed envelope.

Who had sent them? Fritz? He loved lilies-of-the-valley, and had twice given them to me. The Russian lover? Or an unknown admirer—of whom dancers have many? No one would ever know.

I liked to think that they came from her lover, and knowing her, and having heard the caress in her voice when she murmured his name, hoped that she had sometimes found happiness with him.

XIX

Although it was now March the bitter winds were still bringing hail and snow; normally by this time the spring was well advanced, the Berliners told us. This had been the worst winter for over a hundred years—and the spring would be late.

John had not recovered completely from his serious illness and the doctors at Spandau had advised me to take him out of

Germany for at least a month. Somewhere, suggested our nice lieutenant, where he would get fresh fruit and vegetables—things we never saw in Berlin now. In Brussels, the previous November, we had enjoyed every pre-war luxury. The contrast between its overflowing abundance and starving Berlin had been quite horrible; but in Brussels there was plenty of fresh fruit and vegetables and the doctors asked me to take John to the Army Leave Centre there.

On the first really lovely day in March we went out to Gatow. The snow was actually beginning to disappear, except in the deep ditches and dark valleys of the woods. The lake glistened and scintillated like a butterfly's wings in the sunshine. Birds were chattering excitedly in the trees and the children were beginning to shed some of their cocoon-like winter wrappings. I loved this place in spite of the poverty of the little colony of homeless people who were living in shacks round its shores; the relief of the absence of ruins and the beauty of the lake itself were always a solace.

Lilli's death had upset me profoundly. I felt somehow that I had failed her. Every time I played Chopin I saw her little figure in its transient grace flitting across the floor. She had loved to improvise steps while I played.

We walked round the lake to visit Frau von R. and her husband. She had written me an extraordinary note when John was ill.

"If I were logical," it ran, "I would wish that your son should die as mine have done, but on searching my heart I find that I do not wish this—indeed I love your little boy who brings back to me something of the childhood of my Peter and Ernst. It is a bitter world—and for myself I wait only for death to take me out of it. If I believed in God—which I do not—I would pray that He spares your son, but believe me when I say that I wish it with all my heart."

With this note had come some new laid eggs from her few hens and some apples which she had stored from the previous year's crop. I had not seen her since John's illness and was anxious to thank her for her gifts.

They were at home. The packages which we had brought were, as usual, put on a table and deliberately ignored. Dr von R. was still having trouble in getting his de-nazification through the courts.

There was, complained Frau von R. bitterly, a great deal of corruption going on over those courts. If one could pay large bribes one was automatically purged of one's former offences. No honest people could have large sums of money in these days. It was said, she continued, that the Nazis had been corrupt—probably some of them were—but how much worse it was now without them! Had I heard that the Russians had done away with all this de-nazification business? They were far more conscious of the future than we were.

We told her that things would sort themselves out, that it was inevitable in this chaos that corruption flourished, but that the Allies were trying to bring in a currency reform which would soon put an end to the racketeering and black market.

Frau von R. doubted it, and said gloomily that by the time it was brought in, all decent honest people would be dead of starvation and Germany would be peopled and ruled by the corrupt ones.

I had brought her some English periodicals and papers. She thanked me perfunctorily for them, but I knew from her husband that she was really delighted with literature of this kind. She had the same intense interest in our Royal family as had Frau Altmann and Frau Pfeiffer. They considered the German blood in it entitled them to this interest. Princess Elizabeth and the possibility of her marriage to Prince Philip were burning subjects to them.

John was playing with her little dog, and she was asking him about our dogs and the kitten, Puffin.

When we got up to leave she went to a cupboard, and put a flat box in my hands.

"This," she said, "is my greatest treasure, but if it were found in this house now that my husband is trying to get his de-nazification through, it might cause trouble for him. We are forbidden to possess these books, you know."

I took the box without opening it.

"I can't like you," she went on; "life is too bitter for that—but I respect you—and I want *you* to have this and no one else."

I did not know what "this" was until we got home. It was a beautifully bound book with the gold title, *Adolf Hitler*, and depicted in photographs the entire life of the former Führer, from childhood to his rise to fame.

It was a most interesting document, and as my husband said, probably one of very few now in existence, as the Allies had ordered them all to be burned.

We spent the evening poring over the face of this man born to rise with such speed to such heights, and after causing havoc and misery all over the world, to crash to such an ignoble end. A small man—and not a handsome one—but with eyes which, as many Germans said, were magnetic.

I had been going round the wards again with Dr Annemarie. There were many new little faces, but not so many cases of frostbite and cold. Crates were beginning to arrive from Canada now, and the car in which I had come had been filled with blankets, tinned milk, vitamins and cod liver oil, as well as nappies and woollies. Dr Gaupp was making her round of saying good-night to every child.

I thought how much homelier and easier it was for those small mites, coming into a strange place away from their mothers, to be able to address all the doctors as *Tante* and *Onkel*. The contrast in the way the small patients were received on admittance was striking to the way my five-year-old son had been treated in the Military Hospital. I had also been struck with the kindness and gentleness with which Lilli had been nursed. Strange that these people, who could be so gentle and soothing to the sick and could help the dying so mercifully on their last journey, could belong to the same nation as those who had been so revoltingly cruel in the concentration camps. Were they really two-faced? Had they two sides to their character? These questions were forcing themselves upon my mind.

The Berliners could laugh easily like Londoners, and some of the ironical notices they had put on their ruined homes reminded me very much of the days of our London Blitz.

"All my own work—Adolf Hitler" was one I saw, and "Give me ten years and you won't recognize Berlin, Oh yeah!" was another on a completely demolished home. In spite of the acute shortage of food and fuel and the hopelessness of the future their spirits rose as the cold gave way to milder days with the promise of spring.

The complete absence of shops was something which the Allied and German women felt. There was scarcely a single shop left standing in Berlin. The great stores and emporiums lay in dust, as did the great blocks of flats. One could not get the simplest articles except on the Black Market, and then only in exchange for cigarettes and coffee which had taken the place of money. One heard the most witty jokes and verses about the lack of everything. One of them ran something like this: "If I had an onion, I could make some soup. If I had the soup I could put some bread in it. But as I haven't got the onion or the soup I must just live on the smell of them; and watch my stomach shrink!" Ursula had told me of many such verses—she was always well up in the latest Berlin jokes.

We had to receive many of our quadripartite friends before John and I were to leave for Brussels. I had wanted to invite the lovely Baroness B. She was often in the night clubs with her handsome Russian Colonel and I saw her sometimes with her English Bill. Apparently she was quite capable of handling them both. I wrote and invited her, but no answer came. On the day of the party she telephoned me, asking if any Russian guests were coming. I noticed that her voice was a little anxious, but was obliged to tell her that there would be several Russian guests. She said that she was sorry—she would adore to come—no one could regret it more than she—but she could not accept—it might make trouble for her if she came.

It was perhaps significant that after this I was rung up on several occasions by some Soviet official who, after asking my name and verifying the number, would apologize and ring off without giving any name or reason for the call. Gisela became quite worried after this happened. I think it was probably the Russian Colonel who had seen the invitation card.

XX

I HAD NOT seen much of Frau Altmann since Lilli's death. She had seemed so utterly immersed in her grief that I had hesitated to intrude on it.

Ursula, however, came to see me a great deal now. She had been sobered by her sister's death, and seemed to find some comfort in talking about her to me. I encouraged her in this, for it was evident that even if she had been jealous of the adored younger sister, she was missing her terribly and had loved her.

She did not laugh so often or so whole-heartedly as before—and I was surprised when she told me that she was thinking of marrying Joe. They were making plenty of money on the Black Market and were changing it into gold and jewellery she said, which they could sell in the States. Americans were forbidden to marry Germans unless they left the country within forty-eight hours of the marriage. Joe had applied for compassionate shortening of his service and planned to marry her just before he sailed.

"And do you love him?" I asked her.

She smiled in a sceptical way. "I want to get out of this dead-pan place—and Joe's a good guy and he's crazy about me," she said.

"And your mother?"

"Oh, Joe's willing for her to come along too," she said carelessly. "She'll have to," asserted the girl. "How else can she live?"

Somehow I couldn't see Frau Altmann in the United States. She just wouldn't fit in.

On a sunny morning I went to see her, and found her preparing lessons for her children's class.

There was a calmness in her face which was arresting. She looked as if her troubles had washed over her as a healing rain, and left her with renewed faith and strength.

The look I had liked so much had come back again, and her smile was as lovely as when I had first seen her.

She was glad that I had come—she wanted very much to talk to me, she said. First about Lilli. She mentioned the name without any of the pain with which she had mentioned Kurt's. The child had liked me, she said, just as Ursula had told me. I wished so much that I had known this, I could have helped poor Lilli, but I had not known it.

"I shall never forgive myself about Lilli," she said, "Never! She did not confide in me—her own mother. I failed her very badly."

I said that the child had been so perplexed about her own feelings—she must have been, knowing her mother's feelings towards the Russians; how could she have confessed her love for one of them?

Frau Altmann did not want to pursue this side of the question. She still did not want to believe that Lilli had been in love—that what she had done she had done for love; she preferred to believe that the child had been taken advantage of, if not actually raped, by a Russian.

I thought of the way Lilli had murmured over and over again the pet name of her lover—but I said nothing.

Then about Fritz. She had been wrong about him, too. She saw now that he was not what she had thought him to be.

"A mother does not care to admit that her son is either weak or bad," she said sadly. "God sends us these trials in His own way, and we must bear them. I love my children whether good or bad, and I have tried to bring them up to be good. I am sure that Fritz will come back to me one day."

I reminded her that if he were now working for the Soviets that would be difficult.

"We don't know that he is," she checked me gently, "but if he is, then he has chosen his own path and must follow it until he finds out his error."

"I have lost all my children," she went on. "Only six months ago you saw us all round the lamp in the evenings, all except Kurt—and now I have lost them all. Lilli and Fritz and Pappi too."

"But Ursula," I reminded her; "you still have Ursula."

"Ursula I have lost too," she said, "but to America—the others to Russia. Ursula has no more use for the Fatherland. It is finished, she says, Europe is finished, and the only hope is to go to the States. Perhaps she is right. I have lived through two terrible wars, and it seems to me that only those two powers matter now, America and Russia. You British have beggared yourselves fighting for all you hold dear—your freedom—but is there such a thing?"

America and Russia, she said, were vast, and with their unending supply of human cannon fodder, how could smaller countries such as France, Britain and Germany hope to pit their strength against them? She could see that merely from the struggle for Berlin that was going on now. There was constant trouble. Oskar, she said, had always pointed this out to her. He had been right.

It was the longest speech I ever heard her make, and she apologized smilingly for it.

Ursula wanted to marry this American, Joe. She neither liked nor approved of him—but what could she do?

Would she go to the States with them? I asked later. She said decisively that she would not.

"My place is here in Berlin," she said firmly.

Here she had buried her husband and Lilli, from here her two sons had left her—both of them might return one day. She had plenty of teaching now, and if Ursula went to the States, she would let the girls' room and make a little towards the taxes. She could manage quite well—although Ursula thought that she couldn't.

She asked after John. I told her that he had to go away from Berlin for a few weeks and that I was taking him to Belgium. She thought that I myself was very thin, she said. A change of air would not come amiss for me—it had been a terrible winter for us all.

I left her standing there in the sun at the much repaired front door. Her face had a soft wondering look as she pointed to a bush. "Look!" she cried. "The forsythia is almost out. Take some branches with you. They will open in a warm room."

It was true—the buds showed yellow cracks and would open to full bloom in a day or two. Under the hedge a few crocuses were peeping—relics of that once lovely garden which Herr Altmann had made for his bride.

"It's spring!" she cried, clapping her hands; "the winter is over at last!"

In a few days the lilac buds were green, and suddenly with no warning at all the white world had changed and blossomed to a tender green. The icy winds gave way to softer ones with a faint scent of flowers, and the memory of those deathly winter days was already fading.

We went rambling now in the Grunewald with the puppies and with Hans and Renate, Dr Annemarie's twin children. They had become good friends with John although they were much older.

The old Baron brought me a present. His wife was dead. It was better so, he said simply, she had suffered so terribly. Time hung on his hands without her—he had made a kite for John and produced it shyly. It was the most beautiful kite. Painted with birds and flowers, it was both gay and amusing with its tail of many colours. I told him it was a work of art, far too lovely for a small boy who would soon break it, and that I would like to keep it myself. A delighted smile spread over his face as he asked if I really liked kites. Did I fly them? I said that I adored them and had flown them from childhood. He begged me to give this one to John and he would make me the King of all Kites.

It was the weather for kite-flying, and John and I spent a blissful afternoon flying the Baron's kite in the Grunewald.

As we drove home Stampie said to me, "It'll be Easter next week—just think of it!"

Easter was early this year, and Good Friday fell in the first week of April.

On the second of April Stampie came in excitedly. I was glad to see him looking more like his old self. He had been very quiet and gloomy since Lilli's death, and had been drinking more than usual.

"I've heard from Fritz!" he announced.

I said that I hoped Fritz had written to his mother. He had apparently enclosed a note for her inside Stampie's, being afraid probably to write direct to the house.

"Well," I said, "what does he say?"

"Not much," answered Stampie, handing it to me, "Have a look for yourself."

Dear Stampie,

I have heard of my father's death, and I am sorry but it was better so. He was old . . . and there is no place in the new world for the sick and aged. I am doing well and have been given a good and important job. I have a great deal to learn before I am sent to the School in Moscow for the Course. I am learning Russian. It is a musical language, and I learn easily because I have a good ear. Please do what you can for my mother. It will be difficult for me to keep in touch with her now. Thank you, Stampie, for your kindness to us all,

Fritz.

"Well!" I said. "He is just as selfish as ever. Good job indeed—with the Soviet! What a rotten letter. He doesn't ask about anything—his sisters or his mother."

"Don't forget," said Stampie, "that his letters are censored. Look." He held out the envelope which had indeed been opened and bore the Soviet censor's mark.

"What's the postmark?" I asked curiously, for there was no address on the letter.

"Posted at Leipzig," read Stampie, after a careful scrutiny. "And, oh, by the way, there was something enclosed for you."

He handed me an envelope. It was not sealed and bore my name on it. It contained one of those postcards similar to the one he had sent me for Christmas. This one was of the Dome cathedral—the upper part of the postcard depicting it as it was in 1933, and the lower portion as it was now—a ruin.

Across the centre of the card were the same gaily coloured letters which had read, "Best Wishes from Berlin." But on this one, Fritz had crossed out the "from" and substituted "to" in its place.

At the top right-hand corner of the card were the arms of the city of Berlin—a black bear rampant with a crown above. He had struck this out with red ink, and drawn in its place the hammer and the sickle.

SPRING

1948

ON THE NIGHT of the Furtwängler Concert I called for Frau Altmann. She had, I knew, been a great admirer of the famous conductor. It had been rumoured again and again that he was returning, and at last he was back. Opinion was sharply divided as to whether or not his long absence had been due to British disapproval of his association with Hitler, or to his voluntary exile caused by Nazi disapproval of his championship of Jewish musicians. Whichever it was, he was now returning to the scene of his former triumphs to conduct the first performance of his new symphony. The Staatsoper in the Admiralpalast was packed, and among the huge audience feeling was running high. Some were for, and some were against his return; they had come to hear the symphony, but also to judge for themselves how their former idol had fared during his long absence.

He was given an ovation as soon as he appeared, looking even more gaunt and more like a great scarecrow than ever, but at the first bars of the *adagio allegro* of Mozart's lovely Symphony No. 39, which was to precede his own work, it was clear that he had lost none of his magic. The Berlin Philharmonic Orchestra had been giving magnificent performances under the brilliant conductorship of Celibadache, whom I noticed in the audience.

The Mozart was in my opinion quite exquisitely performed, but the Germans round us were more critical. They all had scores with them, which they followed so closely that the rustling of the pages annoyed me. Music to me is the perfect enchantment, the one real magical escape from the world of reality. To these people it was something different. They knew a great deal about music.

There were comments on the Mozart all round us in the interval. I clearly wasn't up to their standard of criticism yet, for I had found it quite perfect.

"Half of them don't really know much about it," said Frau Altmann when I remarked on this. "It has always been the fashion to be critical of music in Germany. Look. There is Ursula!" She was pointing to a couple some way back in the stalls. The girl was Ursula, but the man with her was a stranger to me. He was very tall, broad-shouldered and dark-haired—that was all I could see.

"He is a second cousin of ours, and spent a great deal of his childhood with us—he was Kurt's greatest friend," Frau Altmann told me when I commented on his amazing good looks. "He has recently returned from England where he has been a prisoner of war."

It was astonishing to see Ursula at a symphony concert, and I said so.

"Since she gave up her music studies, yes," agreed her mother. "But in the old days she never missed a concert. Max persuaded her to go with him. He was mad to hear Furtwängler again."

I had forgotten that Ursula had wanted to become a musician. Her life, as I knew with Joe, was as far divorced from symphony concerts as were the jazz and boogie-woogie she indulged in with him.

"Max is coming to live with us," went on Frau Altmann. "The poor boy has come back to find his father dead—his mother died when he was quite small. He has no home and he is going to have the girls' room."

"And Joe?" I asked.

"It has nothing to do with Joe," said Frau Altmann firmly. Max apparently spoke excellent English and had already obtained a job with the Control Commission. He appeared to have made many friends while he was a prisoner in England and had brought back letters of introduction.

"He seems to like Ursula," I observed, watching their animated faces.

"And I think she likes him," said her mother with satisfaction.

The interval was over and we were all attention for the Furtwängler symphony. It was the 23rd of February. A year had elapsed since old Oskar's death, Lilli's death and Fritz's flight. Frau Altmann was thinner and more worn, but her face with its peculiarly luminous quality was strikingly attractive. She was in deep black still.

The symphony disappointed some of the audience. They applauded politely and generously after the four movements had culminated in the Finale, and gave the composer-conductor many curtain calls, but having witnessed the audiences at some of the recent operas I knew that this one lacked the fiery enthusiasm and wild applause which music can awaken in the German.

"What do you expect? He composed it in Switzerland, so they say," said an old man behind me. "It's like the Swiss, dull and smug, nothing grand about it."

"Like these times—a muddle and a mess. Ach! Give me Beethoven, he never disappoints," said another, struggling into his coat.

"Interesting. But somehow just missed," said a large woman next to me. "What did you think of it? You're British aren't you?"

I said stoutly that I liked it. I liked it very much.

"The British are not a musical race," she said coolly. Frau Altmann thought otherwise. She had been astonished at finding amongst her British pupils a great love and feeling for music. The German music masters at the Study Centre told me the same thing.

"You don't talk about it much, but you feel it," they had said. "Some of these young men are really musical and very gifted."

Frau Altmann had also liked the symphony.

"But he is a very sick man," she commented as we left. "One can see it in his eyes. His soul is sick."

I thought that he had plenty to be sick about. He must have felt worse than I had when he first saw Berlin on his return.

We joined Ursula and her companion Max. He addressed Frau Altmann as "Tante Maria" and was plainly devoted to her. He had black hair and very blue eyes set deep in a lean tanned face. He was intense and virile-looking—the sort of man over whom women go quite mad.

"Max has been over four years in England," said Ursula as she introduced me as a friend of the family. "He speaks beautiful English, much better than mine!"

"But yours is American!" he said laughing as we shook hands. Ursula was laughing too. She looked alive and lovely this evening and somehow softer. Her eyes had a brilliance I hadn't seen in them since Lilli's death, and there was less paint than usual on her face.

We went to a small cafe near the Admiralpalast and had some ersatz coffee. It was very nasty, but it served its purpose, for we could sit there and talk.

I asked Max where he had been in England. After various prisoner-of-war camps he had been put to work on a farm, first in the Lake District, and then in Wales.

He had liked it. He had liked the farmer in Wales who had been very good to him. He had become great friends with the farmer's small sons, and had ridden with them every day. He had taught them both German in the evenings, as well as helping them with their school homework.

"Were they Welsh?" I asked him.

"Not really," he said; "they had bought the farm about ten years before the war and had come from the Bristol neighbourhood."

He pulled a crumpled letter from his pocket and showed it me. It was from the elder of the two little boys.

Dear Max,

It's a rotten shame that you are gone. We miss you very much. Stephen and I are saving up to come to Germany to see you. Rosie is fine, she is not lame any more, but Prince is still very lazy. Primrose has dropped her calf, Daddy says to tell you its legs are too weak. We are sending you some food parcels as we hear there is not much food in Berlin. Auf wiedersehen,

Lots of love from Stephen and Paul.

"Rosie is one of the ponies they ride, and Prince was the horse I rode," explained Max. "They are splendid boys. I miss them too. I was wondering if you could be so very kind as to send a small parcel to them through your Field Post. I have got them some tiny German farm models, but cannot send them through our post; it is forbidden."

I said that of course I would send the things. "But you are a Berliner, you weren't used to country life, were you?"

"Oh yes, I was. I was born in Berlin and went to school here with Kurt, as Tante Maria will have told you, but I spent all my holidays with my uncle in Bavaria where I used to help on the estate. Farm life was not new to me."

Frau Altmann had told me that Max was over thirty now; he had been the same age as Kurt. There were very few men of either his age or physique in Berlin now, but some were slowly beginning to trickle back from prisoner-of-war camps. It was easy to tell those who had been in Canada and the United States; they looked in splendid condition. The ones from Britain were in pretty good form too, those from France were not so good, and the ones from Russia were broken men.

We sat there talking until late. I was intensely interested in Max's reactions to Britain and now to Berlin. At first he would not talk much, but after Ursula had assured him that I really wanted him to talk frankly and was not going to listen as an Occupation official's wife, but merely as an interested onlooker, he opened up and couldn't talk fast enough. He had a most charming speaking voice—something very rare in this land of harsh guttural ones—and a very dangerous asset in a man with his looks.

He told me that he had been astounded at the small amount of work the prisoners had been required to do in England. "We were all astonished," he said. "On my farm there were four of us, and we did far more than we need have because we liked it and the farmer was so good to us."

He had been genuinely shocked at the laziness and unwillingness of some of the British workmen. He gave us many small incidents of their unwillingness to do more than they were absolutely obliged to do. The farm hands, he said, refused to do anything on Sundays except the bare feeding. They had refused to help in such an emergency as when the young heifers had strayed into a field of valuable oats on a Sunday, in spite of the fact that it was plainly their fault that the heifers had got out of their own field. They would down tools when their hours were up, regardless whether it was finished. He couldn't understand such things.

"They talk of nothing but Trade Unions," he said; "but your Government, excuse me saying so, are making a race of very lazy people. Here our labourers and farm hands have to work very long hours and very hard for their wages, which are much lower than yours, and now I hear that you are going to revive all the trade unions in Germany."

I asked him about the food.

"There is always food on farms," he said indifferently. "We got our rations and there were always other things—we were not badly fed, but you British have no *lust*—I use the word in the German sense—in anything that you do; you are moderate to the point of boredom. If you have two ounces of butter on your ration, you eke it out by scraping it on several pieces of bread—the German plasters it all on one piece, enjoys that thoroughly, and lives on its memory until the next one. It is the same with all your pleasures—please don't think that I don't appreciate this moderation in all things—but I don't want to be like that myself."

I asked him if he had belonged to the Nazi Party.

"To the Hitler Youth Party, of course," he said, surprised; he was new to post-war Germany and knew nothing of the fashion now of denying having had anything to do with the Nazis.

"Were you a keen member?" I asked.

He smiled. "Haven't I just told you that I dislike moderation? What I do, I do with my whole heart."

I asked if he knew that Berlin had been so terribly destroyed. "Did you?" he countered—"No. All we heard in England was the daily weight of bombs dropped. It gives one no idea of the real destruction. It was a terrible shock to see my birthplace like this," waving a hand at the ruins all round us.

He was alive, intelligent and not yet disillusioned; it was going to be interesting to see what he would make of life in this shambles of what was once Berlin.

Max had said that he received a great shock when he saw Berlin and its devastation; but in the eighteen months since I had first seen it on that lovely autumn morning it had changed its face a little for the better. Or was it, as Stampie said, that you got used to it?

Looking around one saw great masses of rubble everywhere, but efforts were being made now to clear them away. Some large buildings were being repaired, shops were finding the means to rebuild at least one storey and re-open. Others managed to erect a small shack at the foot of the mound of débris of their former building and to carry on business. All down the Kurfürstendamm there were gay little kiosks and shacks and in the previous summer the striped awnings of the cafés and the geraniums and other flowers made a brave show which was doing wonders for the morale of the populace. Faces were far less yellow and strained. People did not jump so violently at the sound of a horn or a bell.

The children looked a little less like wizened gnomes, although their legs were still pathetically thin. They grew at an alarming rate—upwards like overgrown wheat with no roots. The doctors were watching this with foreboding. Fats were still horribly scarce, as were sugar and any kind of oil. The winter had not been anything like as hard as that of the previous year when so many children and old folk had died of their privations. The birds were slowly returning to the trees. There were robins and every kind of tit at our windows now, and our cat Puffin would sit watching them for hours. A magnificent seasonal programme of opera, ballet and concerts had been within the reach of all the Allied personnel; entertaining was still going on every night. Party followed party, each one vying with the other. The clubs were always packed with diners and dancers.

Operas and ballets hitherto unknown to me had been given night after night, all the Russian ones which we seldom have a chance to see in Britain. *Eugene Onegin*, *Sadko* and *The Queen of Spades* were all new to me, as were *Prince Igor*, *Firebird* and *Scheherezade*. Gluck's *Orpheus* was enchantingly given and Erna Berger was delighting us all as Queen of the Night in *The Magic Flute*.

The long-promised visit of the Moscow State Ballet was the highlight of this season for me. I have never seen anything to equal it for sheer perfection as a whole, and surely this should be the ultimate aim of ballet. Exquisitely matched as to height and technique, the Russian ballerinas were so superbly trained that each and every one could dance any rôle. The precision of the corps de ballet was as flawless as that of each individual performance. The wild exciting music of Prokofiev, Asafiev and Khachaturian, new to me, were intoxicating, as were the superb décor and costumes. The barbaric Tartar, Azerbaijan and Ukrainian dances brought something virile and stimulating to a conception of ballet grown somewhat stale at home. Even the purely classical ballets were imbued with this virility and freshness.

I remembered all that Lilli had told me of this ballet and of Ulanova, the idol of the Soviet audiences. Someone had told her a great deal about Ulanova, and how she had looked forward to seeing her. Several times while watching the ballet, the vision of Lilli's light figure in her white practice dress flitted across my mind.

Marshal Sokolovsky had indeed given his friends a feast when he invited us to this. It was only one of the many magnificent entertainments he provided that winter.

Although there were now teachers from home in the schools, I was still helping with the art there and still teaching at the Army Education Centre.

The *reichsmark* was scarcely worth the paper it was printed on and prices were still fantastic on the Black Market. There was constant talk of a currency reform—the date of which was to be kept a secret because of speculators. It had been delayed by the usual Russian refusal to agree to it.

"It won't make any difference to me," said Frau Altmann, when we were discussing it one evening, "I have no hoard of *reichsmarks*."

She looked pointedly at Ursula and Joe who were sitting in the window doing some kind of sums in a notebook. They had not got married as they had intended the previous summer, because Joe had not found it so easy to get his transfer to the States as he had thought. He could not marry Ursula until he was due to leave Germany, and so they had been obliged to wait. Frau Altmann still did not approve of Joe, but she admitted his generosity and that he and Ursula seemed to suit each other well enough.

The Altmann house was just the same. There was never any money to do the repairs which would make it less draughty and less cold. Ursula and her mother managed somehow with Joe's help. We were sitting there listening to the radio and gramophone and they were trying out new records from the States. Gershwin's *Rhapsody in Blue* was Ursula's latest love. She wanted it again and again.

"Like it?" she asked Max, who was reading.

"I do—and I don't," he fenced.

"That's a darned silly answer," drawled Joe; "either you like it or you don't."

Max said nothing. He was watching Ursula, who was gyrating slowly to the waltz theme in it.

I was watching her too. She seemed even harder after Lilli's death and quite impervious to any suffering or privations. She simply took things in her stride, accepting everything as it came. She did not do this with the calm stoical patience of her mother, who now found greater consolation than ever in her religion, but with the bitter armour of disillusioned youth.

Outwardly she was far more polite and affectionate towards Frau Altmann, but it was impossible not to sense the terrible struggle between these two women, both still bitterly antagonistic to each other but each striving to ignore it in the necessity of living together.

Frau Altmann had said resignedly that she supposed Ursula and Joe might as well make a match of it. "There is no one else for her," she had sighed, "for no German man would want to marry her—she is far too hard and selfish." I was not so sure that she was right.

It was soon after the Furtwängler concert that I first noticed her reaction to Max. She was waiting for Joe to take her to one of their usual night clubs. Frau Altmann and I were going to a German cinema together. Max was writing a letter at the table. He asked her where she was going that night.

"To a new place," she said shortly. She was bestowing great care on her face with the aid of a hand mirror which she held under the lamp. Electricity was still scarce, and at the end of each month the meter showed practically nothing left on the tiny ration. The last few days of the month were usually spent in the gloom of candles, when one could obtain them.

"There are plenty of those," I remarked. "They spring up like mushrooms and disappear as quickly."

I saw Max looking intently at Ursula as she made up her face. "It doesn't need all that stuff, Ursi," he said. "Why do you do it?"

She looked up in surprise and paused with a lipstick in her hand. The light from the lamp and two candles lit up her face in the dark room. Her eyes, her most attractive feature, set at a slight slant in her high-cheekboned face, had mysterious shadows round them which made them strangely compelling. I thought she looked like the heroine of some thriller.

"It may not need it, but it's getting it," she said tartly, and drew in the line of her curving upper lip with the red stick. "Things have changed since you left here," she said, snapping the lid of her powder compact shut. "You are still thinking of the days when the Party forbade German women to use make-up, good German women did not use it. Well, there are no good German women left now—so what?"

The bitterness in her voice astounded Max, who protested, "Why, Ursi, don't snap at me like that. I'm not criticising you. I'm trying to tell you that you don't need all that stuff—you are so lovely without it."

He had risen from his chair and was staring at her. The colour rushed into her face and flooded her neck. I looked from one to the other and the picture of those two faces was imprinted on my memory as if I had painted them. It was the first time I had seen Ursula disconcerted or at a loss. Her hand shook, and the lipstick dropped on the floor. In a moment Max had retrieved it for her and just then Frau Altmann came in with Joe at her heels.

I heard Ursula say in a slightly shaking voice, "What about coming along with us, Max—Joe doesn't mind, do you Joe?"

"Sure, come along. We'll find plenty of janes there, there's no shortage."

He had put his arms round Ursula and tilted her face up to his and deliberately kissed her full on the mouth which she had just painted.

It was this lack of reticence in his love-making which so upset Frau Altmann. She hated it. She was no prude, but she simply couldn't bear this kind of caress being given in the presence of others. Apparently Max couldn't either. I saw his blue eyes narrow, then deliberately turning his back he said quietly, "No thank you, I have no desire to come with you."

The difference which the coming of Max had made in Frau Altmann's life was remarkable. She was typical of German women in that they must have some man to serve. She was like a lost soul when Fritz left, and she had no menfolk to wait on. When this man whom she had mothered as a schoolboy had arrived in Berlin lonely and homeless, and had been overjoyed at finding her again, she had immediately suggested that he make his home with them.

Ursula had not liked this. Her relations with Joe were by no means platonic, and the giving up of her bedroom and the sharing of her mother's meant constant scenes now because of the late hours she kept. She argued that she provided most of the money for the home and she was entitled to her own room in it. Max had insisted that she was right, that he could not accept her room, that the divan in the sitting room on which Fritz had slept would suit him admirably.

Frau Altmann did not agree. To her the male had the first call on comfort. Max, who was paying her well for his board and lodging, was in her opinion entitled to a room of his own.

Max was extraordinarily interested in Fritz. He had known him only as a small child, and simply could not take in the fact that he had become a Communist. At the same time he told me that many of the younger men in the service of the Control Commission were attracted by Communism. Their one topic of conversation was politics, just as Karl's our new driver's was, and amongst them the two great subjects for discussion were Communism and Nazism.

"Democracy doesn't come into it at all then?" I asked him.

"No," he replied in surprise. "We Germans are not democrats. And what astonishes us is that you British should think that we are so willing to accept 'the British way of life' as you call it. Just because we are defeated and occupied it does not mean that our whole natures can be changed to accept something absolutely alien to us. Forgive me if I tell you that much as I respect your nation I find them extremely stupid to think like this. In fact I found in Britain that nice as the people were, and they *are* nice, they have the idea that there is only one way to live and that is the British way."

I began to laugh. It seemed funny. The Germans had done exactly the same in the countries they had occupied, forcing totalitarianism on the people by very much harsher methods than ours. I said as much.

"I don't deny it," he answered hotly, "but when you do the same, why do you set yourselves up to be so much better than any other nation?"

"I can't understand you British," he would say. It was always the same. No one understood us. How often had I been told that in other European and Asiatic countries.

"You see, I have been almost five years in Britain and made many friends. No one treated me as a prisoner of war. Indeed they almost apologized that I was one. I was asked to tea at many houses. People took the trouble to find German literature for me to read. They found people to talk German with me so that I should feel at home. This was incredible to us prisoners. A prisoner doesn't expect to be treated in such a way. You don't hate us at all."

"But why should we hate you? What is the good of hate?" I interrupted.

"You must hate someone. It is healthy. There must be some sharply dividing line somewhere in life. How can you love if you don't hate? This amazing moderation in all things is quite alien to us. We are taught to hate certain things and certain people, and by this only can one assess the value of the things one loves."

I told him that the Christian religion taught us not to hate, and that surely what the people in the neighbourhood he had lived in were doing was carrying out their religious teaching.

"But it wasn't Christianity," he said, with the slow smile which was one of his most attractive traits; "it was just the British way of life."

I discovered later from a German secretary of my husband's that this phrase had become quite a slogan among the Germans.

"Don't do this, or don't do that," they would reprove each other; "it isn't the British way of life!"

We would have endless discussions. He was puzzled and completely at sea. He could not understand that the free speech, thought and political views encouraged at home in Britain were not allowed here under the Occupation. "We were never allowed any of these things under Hitler," he insisted, "and did not expect them, but if you are going to force your way of life on to us, then surely we can have your freedom of speech and press too."

It was useless to try and make him see that all this would come later—that we were still engaged in making some kind of order out of chaos. He had not seen the first appalling confusion after the surrender of Germany. Frau Altmann had seen what our troops had done for the Berlin populace and she told him firmly that he was talking nonsense. She hated political talk of any kind. She had endured a good deal of it in her time.

"If there were no politicians there would be no wars," she always insisted. "People understand each other very well; it is the political parties that make all the problems."

"We have no leader. If only we had a leader," Max would say. Lotte frequently said the same thing. "We Germans are no use without a leader. Hitler did unite us. Without a leader we are lost."

AUTUMN

1948

IT WAS ON my return from an eventful journey to London that I noticed how frail Frau Altmann had become. It was as if I saw her with new eyes. She was not an old woman in actual years, but she had endured a great deal recently and it was telling on her. There had been no news of Fritz since that one letter. He may have been a bad son to her, but he was her youngest—her baby. She was a mother and I could understand that she was still grieving terribly over him.

I was in touch with several families in the neighbourhood of Leipzig, and when a member of one of them came to Berlin to collect some parcels which we could not send, I gave him a photograph of Fritz which Ursula had obtained for me. It seemed unlikely that Fritz would be living under his own name now. Stampie had assured me that there were ways and means of getting new papers and identity cards which I wouldn't know about.

Many of these were forged in the large and notorious displaced persons' camps. These former Nazi concentration camps had a bad name as being the centre of the Black Market and of all kinds of racketeering. They were slowly being broken up, as the inmates were being sent to those countries which would accept them. It was Stampie's opinion that Fritz would either have obtained new papers from this source or that the Russians themselves had fixed him up with a new name and identity for their own purposes. They had been known to do this for Germans if it suited Soviet interests to do so. They had already ended de-nazification in the Russian Zone, and a number of wanted Nazi criminals had taken refuge there. Fritz was a wanted man in our Zone and although I found it difficult to believe that he was of any importance to the Russians, his letter to his mother and the one to Stampie seemed to prove otherwise. My friend from Leipzig promised to look out for Fritz, but he was not sanguine.

The blockade of Berlin by the Russians was now assuming ugly proportions. The tension had been growing ever since Sokolovsky had walked out of the A.C.A. quadripartite meeting on March 20th, after accusing the other three Powers of trying to make the Control Council's position impossible. Russia was in the chair for the month of March and this was the climax of many complaints by her that the three Western Powers were trying to undermine the quadripartite control of Germany.

On the 31st March Sokolovsky warned the Allies that more stringent traffic regulations would come into force with respect to rail and road traffic. He also stated that all members of the Allied Administration in Berlin, both Military and Civil, would have to produce proofs of their identity at the Soviet frontier, and that no baggage except purely personal belongings would be allowed through Soviet check-points unless it was searched by Soviet authorities. This applied to both the entering and leaving of Berlin.

General Brownjohn, the Deputy Military Governor of Berlin, denied the right of the Soviet to enter British Military trains between Berlin and the British Zone, or that they had the right to decide what goods should or should not be taken out of the city.

The train by which I had recently travelled from Berlin on my way to London had been detained at the Soviet frontier at Marienborn. There was only one other British traveller besides myself, and we had both been ordered out of it for questioning as to why we were not in possession of the new visa required by Marshal Sokolovsky. The Americans on the train had them; we had not.

The incident had been very unpleasant, and we had been marched away from the train surrounded by armed guards. The production of a recent invitation card to Marshal Sokolovsky's Red Army Day reception with my husband's and my name on it in Russian had helped matters considerably, and after a careful comparison of the name on my passport they had allowed us to rejoin the train, which we found still in the station with guns barring its progress. I was ordered to go to the Soviet Embassy in London and get the new visa. Without it I could not return to Berlin through the Marienborn checkpoint. At the Soviet Embassy I was told that the visa would take from ten to eleven months to grant. I had been obliged to fly back to Berlin to avoid the checkpoint, and found it in a turmoil at the beginning of April, all rail traffic having been cancelled by the British and United States Authorities and a special airline being operated for passengers and freight from Gatow and Tempelhof airports.

Tension mounted higher when the U.S. took their first reprisal for the stopping of their trains by throwing a cordon round the Soviet-controlled railway system, the headquarters of which were situated in the American sector. The division of the city into four sectors had made several such anomalies—the Soviet radio station in the British sector being one of the most awkward.

The Berliners, although outwardly calm, were now brought up with a shock to realize what the closing of the corridor connecting them with Western Germany could mean. They were thrust into further despair. The last year had shown a slow improvement in many things. Overcrowding was still appalling, as was unemployment, food was still terribly scarce, but one could buy anything "black" if one had money. Simple things were beginning to appear again in the shops, and meat and fat rations were now sometimes honoured. Bread was better, although fuel, except for stolen wood, scarcely existed. The sudden forcing upon them of their perilous position shook them from their apathetic acceptance of conditions.

We were discussing it at the Altmanns' one evening while planes roared overhead. I shuddered at the sound, and said that they reminded me of the Battle of Britain, and that some memories of the Blitz and of being rushed to the air-raid shelter were undoubtedly being stirred in John's memory by them. He would not go to sleep at night.

The radio was on, and we were trying to listen to the news while Stampie and Max endeavoured to mend a chair which had collapsed under Ursula the previous evening. Frau Altmann had remarked acidly that the chair had been strong enough for the family for years and she didn't see why Ursula should have broken it.

"Probably had to take the weight of two," said Stampie with a chuckle. "I bet Joe had something to do with it."

Frau Altmann looked disapproving, but Max's face was expressionless as he put down the hammer and listened to the announcer giving the latest news of the air-lift.

"Looks pretty sticky," whistled Stampie, pausing in his work to demand some glue. "Trouble is that the blokes who made that Potsdam Agreement hadn't learned enough geography."

I reminded him mildly who the makers of the Potsdam Agreement were, but he stuck to his opinion.

"No one could be a greater Winnie-fan than me," he declared, "but I still say that none of them except old Joe Stalin knew their geography—and he knew his all right."

Frau Altmann, who was darning socks, remarked stiffly that there must have been a great many things to be considered in the Potsdam Agreement which Mr Stamp could not possibly understand. She could never get used to our British habit of making jokes about our political leaders, and she said this so disapprovingly that Stampie roared with laughter.

"I stand rebuked, M'm," he said sheepishly, "but the fact remains that your capital is an island in the Russkies' Zone, as you are finding out now that Uncle Joe is displeased with his former allies."

"Former allies!" repeated Max. "Don't forget they were once our allies—that epithet applies to us too."

The radio announcer droned on in his oily unctuous voice which somehow made things as black and ominous as possible.

"Switch it off! I can't stand any more of that sanctimonious soft soap—let's have some music," said Stampie suddenly. He had caught the look of acute naked fear on Frau Altmann's unguarded face and couldn't bear it.

"The British will surely feed us somehow. They are very correct," she said firmly as if to reassure herself.

"I hope they will," said Max, "for certainly no manna is likely to fall from heaven as it did for the Israelites."

But here Max was wrong, for it was indeed from the heavens that the food did come, from planes operated by the Allied Air Force. The planes now roaring overhead were the beginning of that magnificent bridge formed so quickly and so efficiently between Berlin and the outer world. Even as we sat there, Ursula and Joe came rushing in excitedly.

"There's been a plane shot down—a British plane shot down by a Russian Yak fighter just as it was going to land at Gatow!" cried Ursula. Her eyes were brilliant in her excited face.

"No!" breathed Frau Altmann. "It isn't possible—you've got it wrong, Ursula."

"It's a fact," Joe insisted. "Saw it myself with my own eyes when I was out at the airport just now. The plane, it's a Viking of BEA, was just going to land when out of the clouds this Yak lunged at it from underneath and they collided in mid-air. It was no accident—it was deliberate—saw it with my own eyes."

"And the plane?" faltered Frau Altmann.

"Crashed—and all passengers are dead," said Joe glumly. "Gee, I'd like a go at those Russians and teach them where they get off!"

Stampie and I looked at each other. Neither of us believed it; we got up to leave, for he was driving me tonight as Karl was off duty, and we were due at a party where I had to meet my husband. That evening, which was the fifth of April, there was a large quadripartite reception given by a British friend at the Gatow Club. It was a brilliant affair, and our host was, I thought, commendably charming to his Russian guests, although the atmosphere was slightly strained; for Joe's report of the collision of the two planes was fairly accurate. Both had crashed—there were fourteen deaths from the British plane, and the pilot of the Yak had been killed in his crash into the British sector. It was difficult to keep the conversation clear of this burning topic. We were all surprised the next day when Marshal Sokolovsky dined with General Robertson to meet his old friend Field-Marshal Montgomery. True, the arrangements had been made before their recent disputes, but it did the Russians credit that their Marshal kept his date, accompanied by Lieut.-General Dratvin, and we were told that it was a very jolly dinner party.

Stampie had got the evening off to go and "take a look" at Monty. "Tougher than he looks," was his verdict on him. "Just because he's fond of his comforts there's no call to say he's softening the army. I like my breakfast in bed myself—and I like my old cat on my bed."

Stampie had acquired a cat. Its name was Lenin. He had found it in some ruins. It was starving and he had taken it to the Mess. "And now," he grinned, "Lenin follows me around like Mary's lamb."

I asked him why the cat was called Lenin.

"Didn't know its name—tried it with all kinds of names— the only one it answers to is Lenin."

"It must be a Russian cat," I said gravely.

The cat indeed became so rapidly attached to Stampie that he had several times found it hidden in the car he was driving.

The Berliners were very excited about the Viking and Yak incident. I found Dr Gaupp and Dr Annemarie discussing it with the two men doctors when I went on my weekly visit with parcels to the hospital. They had no illusions at all about the truth of the incident, and were positive that the Yak's action was deliberate. They expressed great satisfaction at the news that Mr Bevin had made a statement in the House about it, and that General Robertson had ordered that all passenger planes in future were to be escorted by fighters. At the same time it brought home to them the peril they were in, and the fear of war loomed nearer. Dr Gaupp had been terribly ill this winter, and had undergone a serious operation in the Russian sector. She was thankful that she had returned for her convalescence to her own hospital. The hospital was still full of children suffering from malnutrition and chest complaints, but they were getting supplies of the sulfanilamide drugs now, and also some penicillin, and these were making all the difference. The doctors all expressed concern about the milk supplies now that transport was so vital a question. Their babies depended entirely on milk.

"The British will arrange it," said Dr Annemarie confidently; "there is no need to worry." She was always calm and confident and efficient, and soothed everyone's fears by her cheerfulness. The planes filled the sky with their drone, day and night, as they flew backwards and forwards with their freight of food, and from the airports at Gatow and Tempelhof fleets of lorries waited to carry it to the populace.

II

THE FEELING of intense excitement was heightened from day to day by repeated incidents and disputes over the Berlin question. People in the streets had a new look of fear and strain on their dispirited faces, but they were calm and very restrained in their comments. In the homes, arguments and disputes were more open, and there were fierce ones in Frau Altmann's between Ursula, Joe and Max. Joe, who had been put on to airlift duties, was now frequently at Frankfurt, although he was still stationed in Berlin. Many of the returned prisoners like Max were in favour of the Allies taking a much more aggressive line, and even thought we should risk war to force the Russians to keep to the Potsdam Agreement. At the same time it was impossible not to notice that they were jubilant that the Allies were now quarrelling among themselves. The innocent game of halma played between the four Powers over the German territory was assuming exciting proportions.

The former Guards officer, Karl, who now drove us in place of Stampie, was eloquent and vehement on the subject. "Why don't you drive the Russians back *now*, before they have had time to recover from the war effort?" he kept urging. "If you leave it too long it will be too late—they have endless resources and are building them up rapidly."

"Give us all some weapons and we'll fight with you to the last man to drive them out of Germany. They're no friends of yours—they're no friends of anyone's. Hitler was quite right to fight them—they are a danger to the whole world."

Karl had never been anything else but a Guards officer, and had never been a member of the Nazi Party. The regular army had hated the Nazis, he told me. I did not think that Karl had been averse to the régime, in fact he said as much. He was violently anti-Russian, and his antagonism came from fear, as

I soon found out. His father and step-mother were in the East Zone, and he had quickly come to Berlin and obtained work with the British because he could not bear to live under Soviet conditions. After our car had once suffered two punctures on the autobahn between Helmstedt and Berlin, and it looked as if we would have to stay in the forbidden Russian Zone all night, I had discovered just how great was Karl's fear of the Russians. He had been utterly craven with terror, unable to think or to do anything until I had given him all the brandy in my flask. Thank heavens John and I had had an Englishman with us. He had forced Karl to pull himself together until help came. Karl was physically a fine young man, standing well over six feet and with broad shoulders and slim hips, but he lacked the courage of the average German, although he had not suffered much during the war. After Stampie heard of the incident on the autobahn he was quick to shut him up whenever he talked about "giving the Germans a gun to help us drive the Russians out of Berlin."

"Tell that to the Marines!" he would say with a grin—and to me he said solemnly, "You don't want to go believing all that he says to you; just take him out in the Russian Zone and see how he changes. Why, he won't drive one yard into the Russian sector if he can help it."

This was true. I had noticed his reluctance to go there when I wanted to go to the Opera or to shop there. He always had a dozen excuses as to why we should not go through the Brandenburger Tor. When I really wanted to go there it was still Stampie who took me. He had been annoyed and upset at having to give up driving us regularly, and still "wangled" it so that he could drive us whenever possible. He was now driving an Intelligence Chief, "all amongst the cloak and dagger boys," he told me whimsically.

"Not," he reflected, "that there is so much cloak about them. They seem to think I'm a ruddy dummy the way they talk as if I don't exist. Do they think I've no bloomin' ears? How do they know I'm not a Communist?"

He didn't like the job, and was agitating to get put on to the fleet of lorries driving the food from the airports.

He had struck up a friendship with Max immediately. They both liked engineering and tinkering about with engines and radio sets, and spent many evenings together in Stampie's Mess where they were building a super wireless set which was to cut out all Soviet interference. Stampie had an enormous attraction for Germans, both men and women—and a gift for friendship. He was, I had discovered, extremely popular with everyone with whom he came in contact, and was still supporting several entire German families.

The British were already moving many of their Governmental departments out of Berlin into the Zone, and this was causing great hardship and even greater fear to the Germans, who were being told on the Russian radio that we were going to evacuate Berlin and leave them to their fate. Until the end of April 1948 it was still possible to get through the Russian frontier post at Helmstedt by the autobahn if one risked being refused exit at the whim of the officer in charge, who might refuse you on two successive days and wave you through with a smile on the third. As cars were not allowed to remain in the Soviet Zone overnight, it meant returning the two hundred kilometres to Berlin and trying again next day if one were refused.

I asked Stampie if he didn't think that Frau Altmann was looking very ill, and he said thoughtfully, "You're right, her collar's getting looser now I come to think of it, and she's very quiet these days."

She was now teaching quite a number of adults as well as taking a children's class, and although it was true that Max had made life much less empty for her, she was, as Stampie said, very quiet. She was not so afraid—her courage always amazed me—but there was something more than the present political situation on her mind. Ursula gave me the clue to what it was when she came to ask me to lend her my camera one afternoon. It was a lovely spring day, and she had a few hours free. I asked her if she had a film for it. Joe had given her several. He was away in Frankfurt and had his camera with him.

I asked her what she was going to photograph, and she replied that she wanted some snaps of her mother and of the house, and that she would like one of me and one of Stampie. She said suddenly, "I shall like them when I'm in the States."

I was astonished; there had been no talk for a long time of Joe returning to America.

"Is Joe going home soon?" I asked.

"His father's sick—and there are other reasons," she said evasively.

"And are you going with him then?"

She nodded.

"When?"

"In about two months," she said laconically.

I asked her if she had told her mother. No, she had not. Joe was going to do that when he returned from Frankfurt.

"And Max?" I asked.

"Max?" she repeated, "what's it got to do with Max?" and burst into tears. Unlike most German girls, she did not cry easily.

Presently she took the camera and went away with it.

On the following Sunday John and I had been walking in the Grunewald with the dogs when Max passed us with his usually good-tempered face looking set and angry. He gave us the most formal of greetings, only stopping to help untangle John's kite-string, and striding on across the heath as if he were pursued by devils.

It was so unlike Max that we were astonished until, further on down by the lake, we found Ursula. She was sitting there on a tree-stump looking at the filthy water. The lake had changed little since the end of the war, but some of the old tanks and guns were gradually being removed. There were still huge and dangerous craters all over the Grunewald, and in some parts there was scarcely a tree left now—all had been ruthlessly knocked down for firewood.

"Have you been quarrelling with Max?" I asked her. "We passed him just now looking like a thundercloud."

She said, "He is quite unreasonable, and now he is furious with me."

John wandered off with the dogs and I sat down beside her. Her face was sullen and her mouth set tight. She was thinner and had faint shadows under her eyes.

I said bluntly, "What's the matter, Ursula?" And when she didn't answer I asked her boldly if it were Max. "You're in love with him, aren't you?"

She said violently, "I'm paying for my sins all right. One has to pay for everything in this world. Well, I'm paying now. Max called me vile names. He says I'm selling myself. What does he know about being hungry and cold? He's never gone without anything, he doesn't even ask where the meat and butter that Mutti puts before him come from. He just takes it for granted. Doesn't he know that those things can't be paid for with money? What right has he got to criticise me?"

I knew that a great deal of the food at the Altmanns' came from Joe, who got it from the U.S. Commissariat. Frau Altmann had never made any comment to me on the matter and always accepted any small gifts of tea or coffee or food which I gave her gratefully, but with dignity. She invariably made me some small return, which I accepted. I knew that Ursula and Joe frequently "flogged" both food and spirits on the Black Market and were thus acquiring quite a collection of valuables to take back to the States with them. Joe obviously did not need money. His family appeared to be well off and he was the only son.

"I wish Max had never come back!" said Ursula stormily, "Everything was all right until he came to live with us."

I said, "You're angry with him because you are in love with him. You wouldn't care what he said if he meant nothing to you."

It was only last year that she had told me there was no such thing as love, and now here she was, caught on the wheel herself.

She didn't answer me for some time; then she said, "It's the first time I've minded about all the others; now I'd give anything to wipe them out."

"And Joe?" I said.

"Joe's a good guy," she said flatly; "I'm not breaking my bargain with him."

"You're going to marry him although you're in love with Max?"

She nodded.

I asked what Max thought about that. She said dully that he had merely expressed the opinion that she would get what she deserved if she married one of the Occupation.

I was surprised. Max had not struck me as being anti-British or anti-American. Apparently he was not, but he had strong ideas on just how far one should go with the Occupational Powers—and marriage was not included.

I asked if Max wanted to marry her himself. She looked at me in surprise, and said quietly, "He wouldn't marry me after all those others. Max is the sort who wants an unchalked slate."

The misery on her face was unbearable. I said that Max had not the right to judge her if he was not willing to help her himself.

"But he is, that's just it. He wants me to get a job in the Control Commission so that I'll earn better money, and give up all this Black Market—and Joe."

"And you won't?"

"I'm going to marry Joe," she said firmly. "He likes me as I am—he's been good to me. Don't let's talk about it any more."

We joined John and the dogs, and she was soon racing about with them as if she hadn't a care in the world.

I thought about her all that evening at a party in the French sector at Frohnau. We were dancing in the Bagatelle Club to a new series of tunes, including the *Rhapsody in Blue*. Our French friends were very indignant over the whole blockade position. They were much less patient than we were, but saw only too well that short of war there was nothing to be done. They were also going to be moved out into the French Zone to Mainz and Baden Baden. The whole Allied Control Commission was going to be dotted about over the zones because of this Russian boycott of the Allied Kommandatura Council. The Allies foresaw a blockade and possible further trouble and had made their plans when Sokolovsky walked out on them.

The blockade of Berlin and the acute shortage of food, combined with the illness of his father, were two of the factors which hastened Joe's departure; there were two more which brought it to a climax. The first was the currency reform which came into force on June 20th, and put a stop for the time being to racketeering and Black Market deals—and the other was Max.

Joe was a quiet person, but he was no fool. He was quite aware of the attraction Max had for Ursula, and he began to resent more and more his frequent absences from Berlin, when she was left with Max. Outwardly unperturbed, and always chewing the eternal gum or with a cigarette hanging from the side of his mouth, he took the situation in and acted. We were sitting with Frau Altmann one evening when he and Ursula dropped a bombshell by saying that they would be getting married in a month or so.

Frau Altmann took it with her chin up. Without a quiver in her voice she inquired if that meant that he would be leaving Germany sooner than he had planned.

"Yeah! that's right, the old man's sick and wants me home— they've granted me compassionate shortening of my overseas service. We'll be getting married almost right away."

"So!" That was all, but there was a wealth of feeling in that "So!"

Ursula jumped up and ran to her mother.

"But you are to come with us, Mutti; Joe has arranged it all. You are either to come with us or to follow on as soon as Joe has arranged your papers from the other side."

Frau Altmann untangled herself from Ursula's arms and said firmly, "No. It is kind of you young people to want to take me with you—but no, I am too old to want to leave my country. I shall stay here and wait for Kurt and Fritz to come home. This is their home. The house is theirs. I have no right to it. If it is empty it will be requisitioned at once or squatters will take possession of it, and one can never get it back again."

She looked at me appealingly. I felt for her. There was but the faintest chance that Kurt would come back from Russia, and the blockade had put an end to her hopes that the feeling between Russia and the other Allies would improve and that Germany would be united so that Fritz could come home to her again.

Stampie changed the subject happily. "What does your Dad do for a living?" he asked Joe.

"Plays around with his meat-canning factory," said Joe, chewing again, "and I'll sure have to do the playing around now if he's sick."

"Does your father own the factory?" asked Frau Altmann.

"Sure—his old man built it up—it'll be mine when my old man is for the high jump—and it sure looks that way now."

"And what is the nature of your father's illness?" asked Frau Altmann.

"Dunno! Old age, I reckon—the old man's nearly fifty."

Frau Altmann got up with the sharp movement which showed her disapproval at the way Joe spoke of his father, but at the same time I caught a gleam of satisfaction in her face at the mention of the fact that Joe was the prospective owner of a factory.

She said stiffly, "You must decide on the day of your wedding, then, so that I can inform the pastor."

"What's it got to do with him?" drawled Joe. "I reckoned to get us tied up at the Attorney's, or Burgomaster's or whatever the rule is here—Ursi and I don't want any fuss."

"I have only one daughter now, I should be sorry indeed if she were to be married without the blessing of the Church." Frau Altmann's voice was like ice.

Ursula's face was mutinous, but Joe, whose patience seemed as inexhaustible as his good nature, put a hand on the old woman's arm.

"Now, now, you don't want to take on, Mam, it's all the same with me. I don't reckon to belong to any religious denomination, but if Ursi likes Mother Church, well, I guess she's entitled to the old lady."

"It takes two, you know, to get married. Ursula can't just go along there by herself," Frau Altmann said acidly.

Joe looked bewildered.

"Sure, aren't I telling you—I'm going along all right, I'm telling you folks that what Ursi says goes with this guy, see?"

Frau Altmann picked up her knitting. "In my country the husband gives the orders. His wishes are law," she said firmly.

"Well, in the States we reckon to let the skirts do the boss-ing—we just tag along and pay." Joe's voice held just the faint-est edge of impatience now. He was easily bored and had al-ready talked a great deal for him.

"Mutti!" cried Ursula despairingly, "please do let us do things as we like. The world has changed—it is changing every day. People don't make such a fuss any more about getting married."

"There is no need," was her mother's dry comment, "when in the country to which you are going a marriage need last only a few months. That is why it is probably fashionable to dispense with the Church."

I saw Ursula flinch, but her eyes were angry.

Frau Altmann was getting bitter now, I thought, and bitter-ness was a quality she had never shown me before. Was it that she could not like Joe? Or was it the natural antipathy between this daughter and herself?

It was that evening that Stampie came to see me. Gise-la came in at dinner and said that he was outside and was very mysterious, but wanted to see me urgently.

I was alone and asked him to come in. He looked ill at ease until I put a brandy in his hand.

"This is the stuff!" he said, drinking it down in one gulp, "but not as good as Danziger Lachs. Have you ever tasted it?"

I shook my head.

"Bring you a bottle tomorrow," he said, "but mind how you drink it—it affects your eyes. Funny thing, I see the world on a slant after that stuff. Perfectly normal world, but on a slant."

I said it would interest me as a painter to see the world at such an angle. He talked of this and that and then came to the point of his visit. He had come to tell me, he said, that there would be a few things coming for me the following day. I was not to be surprised. The fact was, he had heard rumours—persistent rumours—that there was to be currency reform, he was not taking any risks. He was spending all his reichsmarks.

I asked him if he had many.

"Not now," he grinned; "I've bought solidly for the last five days. Now I'm nearly cleared out—they can bring in currency reform tomorrow for all I care."

I suggested that the rumours might be false, in which case he had spent all his money.

"No matter, there's plenty more where that came from." He fidgeted a moment, then asked me sheepishly if the Boss, as he still called my husband, would know anything about the date of currency reform.

I told him firmly that I knew nothing—my husband would not dream of telling me such a thing even if he knew it himself.

"About these things," he continued, "there's some plants and knick-knacks—oh, no value," he said hastily as he saw me about to protest, "and some things for John—trains and things."

It was no use arguing with him. He sat there playing with the cat and the dogs, who were still all three great friends; then asked if he could see John, who was in bed but not asleep.

The next day "the things" as he called them began arriving. He had been very clever. There was absolutely nothing that did not come within the prescribed rules for the Occupation Forces. The thing I liked best was a jacket made of floor cloths with many pockets and wooden buttons, which had been made to my measurements. It was extremely smart. Lotte told me that he had asked her for my measurements, explaining that he didn't like to see me in such dirty painting overalls, and when I remonstrated with him for it, he explained glibly that he knew a "little girl" who made these jackets for a living, and that he had been doing her a kindness by giving her an order. Gisela liked it so much that she went to order one for herself. The "little girl" was a buxom and attractive blonde who was managing to feed her two children by the making of these original jackets. She sat and talked about Mr Stamp to Gisela for an hour. She thought that next to Herr Hitler he was the greatest man in the world.

A few weeks later Stampie was proved right in his premonition, and everyone woke up to the news that the reichsmark was no longer of any value or negotiable. There was a new Deutsche Mark now, and the first issue of forty marks for each person was to be made through the food offices upon presentation of ration books and identity cards. There was no discrimination. Everyone got forty marks and that was that.

There was dismay, astonishment, disbelief and anger, all to no avail. Furthermore, the full forty marks were not all given out at once. People had got so accustomed to paying huge sums in reichsmarks for simple necessities that forty marks seemed at first a pittance. All reichsmarks had to be handed in. It was possible that a payment might be made at a later date of one mark to ten.

Two other people who had been buying hard in the week before the change were Joe and Ursula. I went with Ursula to one of the most elegant dress salons I have visited anywhere in the world, to choose her wedding dress.

Seated on pale silver-grey velvet chairs, our feet on a pale grey carpet at least two inches thick, we watched some really beautiful mannequins parade for us in the latest creations of Kurfürstendamm. It was incredible to think that one was in Berlin. The prices were fantastic, but Ursula was quite undaunted by them. Supplied by Joe with great wads of notes, she sat like a queen casting a critical eye on each model as its wearer glided past. She might have been born to this world, I thought, as she tried on one or two which we liked. "Wouldn't they be surprised if they knew that an hour ago I was washing dishes?" she giggled as an exquisite gown was slipped over her head.

"I can do it like those mannequins too," she said delightedly as, arrayed in this creation, she turned, twisted, and preened herself in the galaxy of mirrors.

We chose a dress of a soft mushroom grey-pink. There was a matching coat, and a little cap of flower petals. Ursula looked absolutely charming in them. She decided on black gloves and a silver fox fur to wear with it. Joe, she said, wanted her to look nice. He had invited a number of his friends, including his commanding officer, to their wedding.

I asked her what had finally been settled, and heard that there was to be a legal ceremony followed by a church one. "Neither Joe nor I want the church ceremony," she said, "but we can't upset Mother."

And now one could buy nothing on the Black Market. The shops were empty—they were taking no chances and were holding back their stocks until they saw which way the cat was going to jump. The Black Marketeers were also chary. It was no use their accepting the old useless currency, and they were doubtful if the new one would survive, for the Russians were denouncing it in a violent newspaper and radio campaign. They had begun the campaign well before the new mark was launched, with General Sokolovsky's violent denunciation of the separate money reform on June 18th. The other three Powers, tired of their fruitless efforts to come to an agreement with Russia, had formed a tripartite administration in place of the former quadripartite at the A.C.A., and the new currency was the result. The electricity plant for the city unfortunately lay in the Russian sector, and the angry Russians plunged the other sectors into darkness. The Berliners, only too used to groping about in candle-light from the endless electricity cuts in the past years, now found it impossible to get any candles, for the shops would not part with their stocks until they saw the results of this new Russian crisis. We groped about in the light of the Christmas tree candle-stumps, for the Naafi supplies soon ran out. People went about with lanterns, and the Army delivered two enormous hurricane paraffin lamps to each household without a supply of paraffin for use in them. As usual Stampie came to everyone's rescue with an unending supply of yellow tallow candles.

"Very holy, these are," he told me. "They send the prayers up quicker to the Almighty than any other kind."

Frau Altmann was scandalized, but she accepted them just the same. The British retaliation for this Stygian darkness, the stopping for the flow of steel and metal goods from Berlin into the Soviet Zone, brought back the power again to a city now resigned to anything.

The British were moving out branch after branch of their Government into the Zone, as were the French and Americans. The Soviet radio and the *Tägliche Rundschau* were quick to take advantage of these moves to report that we intended to evacuate Berlin and leave the Berliners to the Soviet, and although this was refuted by the Foreign Office, much damage had been done to our prestige with the Germans, which of course was the Soviet's intention.

It was difficult to calm the fears of the mothers and children at the Fürsorge. They did not read much, but they listened to the radio news, and unfortunately many of the Soviet-controlled programmes cut through ours. They had not forgotten the horrors of the sack of the city, and wanted reassurance that the British and Americans would not leave them to their fate. Dr Annemarie was through all this crisis calmly confident and placidly reassuring. Dr Gaupp had left for a large hospital in Stuttgart. Her doctors considered that Berlin would be too great a strain on her for complete recovery. She wrote happily from her new work, telling me how very generous and helpful she found the American authorities in her dealings with them. She was head of a very big children's hospital and loved it.

Throughout all this wrangling and the constant alarms and crises, we were still going out with our Russian friends and they coming to us. The only difference was that the entertaining was now private. The large-scale Russian receptions and parties had ceased, and we gathered from our friends that they were not encouraged to be on too friendly terms with us now. Nevertheless we enjoyed some splendid evenings with them, at which the subject of the blockade was strictly taboo.

Frau Altmann was upset and agitated one day at receiving a letter from her youngest sister in Breslau. They had two children, and although the Altmann family were constantly sending small parcels they received the briefest of letters of thanks, with very little news. This letter, which had been brought to Berlin by a friend from Breslau, told Frau Altmann that her brother-in-law had been taken away from his home for "work for the Soviet Five Year Plan," and that she and the two children were in a pretty poor way. The brother-in-law was a scientist, apparently a very useful one to the Russians.

III

URSULA HAD WANTED one of my paintings for her wedding present, and I had done a head of her. I was not satisfied with it, for although a fair enough likeness, it was too static and set for anyone with her changeable and volatile nature. She and Joe were delighted with it, however, and having with difficulty found a frame for it I took it down to her one evening two days before the wedding.

I had grown to like Joe. His devotion to Ursula was absolute and complete.

"She's the sort of girl who gets under your skin," he had said to me on one of the several talks I had with him, "and I know right now I'll never want any other."

I had asked him how his parents, who were people of substance, would feel towards her. He was their only son.

"Mum knows all about Ursi," he said, surprised. "I've written right from the beginning that I wanted to marry her and bring her home to the States—she'll give her a grand welcome when we get there. Mum's all right."

"And your father?" I asked.

"He's real glad that I'm settling down and coming home to take over the factory," said Joe. "He'll love Ursi. He can appreciate a pretty skirt same as me."

"You like her, don't you?" he asked.

I said that it was because I liked her that I was asking—life had knocked Ursula about quite enough—and I would like to know that she was going to be happy in her new home.

"It won't be my fault if she isn't," he said earnestly. "She can start a new life out there and forget all the past—she's a grand girl—she's too good for me. I'll never let her down."

He wouldn't—I felt that, and I had told Frau Altmann so.

I had not intended to do more than hand the package containing the painting to Ursula, but when on my arrival Frau

Altmann drew me insistently in, I sensed at once that there was a crisis. Max and Joe sat silently on each side of the table in the sitting-room. Ursula was in her room. She had locked herself in and refused to admit anyone. There had apparently been a scene, but her mother did not enlighten me as to the cause, merely begging me to go in and see Ursula.

"She will admit you," she insisted, and knocking on the door called out imperatively that I had brought her portrait and would she kindly remember her manners and let me in.

There was silence and then the door was opened.

Ursula had been lying on her bed, her hair was tumbled and wild, her face tear-stained and dirty.

"What's the matter?" I asked, shutting the door carefully behind me.

A storm of tears was the answer, and she flung herself back on the rumpled bed and gave way to violent sobbing, and in this sobbing was something deep and wretched. I sat down and waited. Presently she sat up and began talking. Once started the words poured out in violent jerky spasms, punctuated with sobs.

There had been a scene between Joe and Max. They had come to blows. Joe had resented a remark which Max had made about the forthcoming marriage, and ordered him to take it back. Max had refused, saying that he had been disgusted at the servility of his fellow-countrymen to the Allies, but that he felt differently and that he was not going to apologize.

Joe had taunted him with being only too glad to take their money and food, telling him that most of the food he ate came from America. They had come to blows, and Ursula and Frau Altmann had been terrified. It was unheard of for a German to express such opinions to a member of the Occupation, and furthermore it was very dangerous. Ursula had got between them and forced them apart, but in the struggle she had inadvertently received a blow from Max, which had infuriated Joe. Frau Altmann had been too horrified to intervene, but had insisted that Max either apologize or leave her house. He had apologized very reluctantly, but Joe had taken it very decently.

"Aw, forget it," was all he had said, offering his hand with a grin.

No one had been deceived as to the real issue, which was Ursula. Max, even if he were not willing to marry her himself, could not bear Joe to have her. It was not really the fact with which he had taunted her—that she was marrying one of the Occupation—that rankled, but that another man was getting her.

"Max is impossible," sobbed Ursula. "Mutti adores him."

And here lay another cause of the trouble. Ursula was jealous of Max just as she had been jealous of Lilli. Her mother had always denied her the affection and consideration which she had given her brothers and Lilli. For some reason which she probably did not understand herself, Frau Altmann did not really like Ursula.

I let her run on until it was all out and she was completely exhausted, and then I asked Frau Altmann for a cup of tea for her.

"And now what?" I said mildly when she had drunk the tea.

She said wildly, "Max doesn't want me himself, but he won't leave me alone. He says disgusting things to me—he's always condemning me, and he gets letters from a girl in England. She's as pure as the snow, I suppose, and that's what he wants."

"An English girl?" I asked.

"No, an Austrian girl he met at a farm there," she said dolefully.

"And you are in love with Max, aren't you?" I said.

She burst into fresh sobbing.

"And you are still going on with this marriage with Joe?" I persisted.

She nodded vehemently. "Yes. I want security, it's no use staying here. Joe's had all the joys of the marriage bed, why shouldn't I have the ring and the marriage licence? It is all finished here, there is no future here."

"No future here." How often one heard that now on every hand. Every woman was trying to get away, to get out anywhere—to start afresh. So many wanted to go to Australia, to

Canada, to South America, and later on perhaps they would be able to go—they had been told so.

Ursula couldn't have it both ways. There was Joe with the dollars and Max whom she loved.

I said, "If you really love Max you can get him—any woman can get the man she wants if she really tries."

"Not Max," she said bitterly. "He doesn't love me. So what?"

I thought of Lilli who had lain in this room, and of what she must have suffered, She had had courage, that one, more than Ursula had. As if reading my thought, she said,

"Lilli was in love too, and look where it got her. No. The other thing is much better."

"What other thing?" I asked curiously.

"Oh, just tagging along with Joe," she muttered.

"You've never known the real thing, Ursula," I said gently. "So how can you judge?"

She was calmer now and got up to bathe her face. There was an ugly bruise coming up where she had received Max's blow. We debated what to put on it.

"I don't want to speak to Max again," she said brokenly as she looked in the mirror. "I hate him, hate him, *hate* him!"

I V

THE WEDDING went stormily from the start. There had been a wrangle over those black gloves and the silver fox. Frau Altmann had ordered the traditional myrtle wreath, although Ursula had declared that she would not wear it. She had implored Ursula to substitute white gloves for the black suède ones. She had never heard of a bride in black gloves; it was horrible, she declared. The orchids were the last straw. A bride should carry lilies or roses or carnations—but orchids! And such queer coloured odd-looking ones at that. Ursula had refused to make any alterations in her outfit. She had seen a picture of one of her favourite American film stars in just such a scheme as hers and she was going to have it as she wanted. As to the orchids, all her life she had longed for some, and Joe had searched Berlin for them. It was, of course, Stampie who had found them. They were always obtainable at one of the most expensive florists, but now with the acute fuel shortage and the money muddle, there had not been any about. Stampie had gone to old Heinrich who knew where to get them. I thought they were lovely in their fragile butterfly beauty, and their queer greenish-brown-pink was just right for both the dress and Ursula's colouring. She was an unusual looking girl with her strange-coloured hair and slanting greenish eyes, and she had never looked more attractive than she did in her wedding clothes, in spite of the bruise on her cheek. It still showed although she had done her best with cosmetics.

The civil ceremony took place in the morning and was attended only by Frau Altmann and Joe's best friend, Sam, a fellow-Sergeant in the U.S.A.F.

Frau Altmann had insisted on Ursula's walking in the traditional style from her home to the church on her bridegroom's arm, and had planned the procession of guests with great care. Joe hated walking; he said he hated to be made to look a fool, and what was the use of having the car if one had to walk to one's wedding?

His car was a converted jeep and its springs were practically non-existent. He had put some cushions in it, and he and Ursula found it comfortable enough.

All Frau Altmann's plans for the bridal procession were ruined by the weather. The day, which had dawned sunny and warm with a cloudless sky, changed at midday. Thunder began in great long rumbles, the blue of the sky turned rapidly to a strange livid grey-green, and streaks of forked lightning illumined the outlines of the huge banks of clouds.

Five minutes before the bride was due to leave for the church the heavens opened and a wall of water poured down on Berlin. She could not possibly walk, nor could anyone else. Joe picked his bride up with a complete lack of ceremony and dumped her on a rug in the front seat of the jeep.

"Come on folks! Pile in!" he yelled, holding his raincoat over his head, and to Frau Altmann's horror the young people who had assembled for the procession tumbled into the back of the jeep, with shrieks of merriment, sitting on each other's knees and making the best of discomfort. Frau Altmann and her sister-in-law came in the car which had been lent me, and we picked up John on the way. He was terribly excited at going to a wedding and did not appear to notice the thunder. I had not wanted him to come, but Ursula had begged for him, as it was considered very unlucky not to have at least one child at a wedding.

I asked where Max was, as I had not seen him at the house. He had gone to the church with Stampie, said Frau Altmann. At first he had blankly refused to attend the wedding at all. He and Ursula had not spoken to each other since the scene two nights before, but Joe had begged him to come, and he had finally agreed to go with Stampie.

"It's all so difficult," sighed Frau Altmann. "I don't understand the young people nowadays in the least—they speak a different language from ours." The storm depressed her even more—it was surely a bad omen for this marriage. I said that probably by the time Ursula came out of the church the sun would be out.

The roof of the church, which had been blown in during the Blitz, had been covered with corrugated iron. The noise of the torrential rain was so deafening that not a word of the service could be heard. The church was so dark that it was not possible to see, let alone read, and the whole thing was inconceivably depressing. It was cold too, for the building had not been heated all the winter, and an icy chill seemed to emanate from its battered walls in spite of all the sun of the previous weeks. John was disappointed. He had pictured a fairy-tale wedding, and here in this dark church he was frightened and miserable.

At last it was over—there was no music and, except for the flowers in the church, nothing to suggest a wedding at all. The young couple seemed quite unperturbed by the gloom and incessant echoes of the rain on the tin roof, and Ursula was smiling and radiant as she received the congratulations of her friends as they trooped to the church door.

I was wrong, the rain had not abated in the least; if anything it was worse. As we waited in the porch there was a tremendous crash of thunder which reverberated from the roof overhead, and a brilliant flash of lightning illumined our faces. Stampie was at that moment taking the opportunity of kissing the bride, and addressing her by her new married name. Ursula's charming upturned face was suddenly ringed with light, as was Stampie's saturnine one as he bent to kiss her. I caught a glimpse of Max's face too; he was looking at Ursula and it was completely unguarded. He had not expected that flash any more than had any of us. His feeling for Ursula was written there for all to see, but Ursula's back was turned to him, and everyone was looking at the bride.

The wedding reception in the home was, from necessity, very simple. The young people were all going on to dine and dance at an American club afterwards. Ursula and Joe were leaving by plane in the early morning for Frankfurt, from where they would travel to Bremen.

The storm showed no sign of ending, and Joe put on the radio to drown the rain. In that small room the wedding cake was on a table with the stars and stripes flag under it as a table-cloth. The idea had been Ursula's in honour of her new country. She had wanted to cover the walls with U.S. flags, but her mother had said firmly that it would be an insult to her German guests, and that one under the cake would be sufficient. Ursula never did anything by halves. She would, I thought, adopt everything typical of her new country, just as she had adopted its hair fashion and face styles, its music and its dances. She seldom spoke German now, declared that she could no longer read German literature—it was all too long-winded and pompous. She was not taking a single German book with her except a childhood copy of *Struwwelpeter* which she loved.

Frau Altmann had been terribly concerned about her not having the traditional treasure chest of linen. She had put aside huge sets of everything for both her daughters, but owing to the bombing and the looting and the impossibility of renewing her own household linen for the past ten years, most of it had gone. Ursula had, however, still received what most modern girls would think a large stock of linen, which had already been sent to her new home.

There was champagne provided by Joe, and we drank their health. Was it an accident that the glass slipped from Max's hand just as he was about to drink? Another quickly took its place, but watching him I saw that he did not drink it, but only put it to his lips and then poured it into Stampie's ever-empty glass. Then Joe had put on Ursula's favourite record of *Rhapsody in Blue*. The incident made me uneasy. He was a strange deep man, this Max, who had spent four years in my country and had gathered from it such disconcerting ideas. His deep-set blue eyes were expressionless now until they lit on John, standing delightedly by the bride and helping her to cut the cake. She had put an orchid from her bouquet spray into his buttonhole, and he had tasted some champagne and was wrinkling up his nose as the bubbles tickled him. Max's eyes softened as they took in John's eager little face. He loved children, and missed the two small sons of the farmer on whose land he had worked.

It was stiflingly airless in the small room with so many people and the gramophone blaring and the rain deluging down. I thought that if I stayed much longer I should faint. Stampie caught my eye and, speaking to Frau Altmann, opened one of the windows. The noise of the rain was even worse, but no one noticed it in the chatter and laughter.

Ursula had put her portrait out on view, and it was much commented on. Some thought it like her, and some did not, but artists are too accustomed to such controversies to be anything but amused by them. Max said to me, "It is a very good portrait of Ursula, and you have caught some of her loneliness and unhappiness in spite of the smiling eyes."

I was startled, because it was just this which had prevented me from getting the gay irresponsible Ursula one usually saw. The portrait had something too deep and set in it for Ursula, and yet these qualities had been there and had, in spite of my efforts, superseded the more superficial ones.

He said, "I would like to possess it," and turned away.

We left soon afterwards. I could see that Frau Altmann was very tired and could not stand much more. The noise and constant jiggling about from one foot to another of the guests in time to the swing music from the radio, their jokes which had no meaning for her, their references to events and incidents in their night life, in which she had no part, were not only out of place but ill-judged.

Stampie hustled them off, promising to join them later on, as I had done. We wanted to get them out of the house before Frau Altmann collapsed, which it was obvious she was going to do very soon. She was terribly pale, and great beads of sweat were on her forehead, but she was too well-bred to dream of excusing herself and going to lie down. She could never stand thunderstorms, she told me. She found them unbearably oppressive, and if they went on for long she invariably became really ill. Max was by her side constantly, bringing her water several times, and once a little brandy. She refused to sit, and continued to stand until the bridal couple were escorted with much noise and laughter to the jeep, the guests holding the stars and stripes flag, which they had pulled from under the cake, over their heads as a canopy from the rain. Only then did she sit limply on a chair and allow her sister-in-law to bathe her forehead with eau-de-cologne.

"She is married," she said in a heart-broken voice. "There are no children left," and now that the guests were gone she wept unashamedly.

V

ALTHOUGH THE NEW currency had more or less settled down now, people were resentful at having lost their savings again, and without any kind of warning.

The shops no longer wanted cigarettes and coffee—they wanted money—the new money, and to get it they began releasing the stocks of goods which they had hoarded against just such a happening.

Great was the indignation of the housewives at some of the shopkeepers.

"Just look at all these buttons, fasteners and elastic which have suddenly appeared," said one to me, "and the needles and pins. They are all old stock—the wretches must have been hoarding them up for years."

Clothes appeared—all kinds of clothes and shoes—and household goods which had been missing from the market for years began to fill the shop windows. But now that their pockets were empty—for the miserable forty marks had not been all paid out at once—these women were in a veritable fury and loud in their contempt of the shopkeepers.

The Russians took full advantage of this, having launched their own currency, known as the East Deutsche mark, at the end of July, and the battle of the marks was now added to the battle to force the Allies to relinquish their rights and to give up the city.

Planes droned over day and night—Skymasters, B.E.A. liners, Dakotas, Lancasters, Tudors—and the air was noisy with their engines as they brought in more and more food and fuel to the blockaded city. Fear lent strength to the Berliners in their determination to resist the Russian campaign. They minded the new food shortage less because everyone was in the same boat—the Allies were as strictly rationed as they were, and with fuel too. One of the greatest grumbles in the previous winters had been the complete absence of fuel for the Germans and the abundance enjoyed by the Occupation. It was warm still, but the evenings were already getting chilly. The September days were golden and sunny, but there was no relaxation for the populace who, although still sunbathing and deepening the tan of their misleadingly healthy-looking skins, watched the planes in the sky anxiously, and worried about the safety of their life-line.

It was on one of these glorious September days that Stampie was driving me through the Charlottenburg Chaussée when we came upon an ugly crowd throwing stones at Soviet sentries who had arrived to take over the guard at the Red Army War Memorial. They were in our sector, but as their War Memorial was situated in the British sector they had a perfect right there. Why the crowd had decided to attack them was not clear, but it was probably the pent-up feelings of the Berliners coming to a head and finding release in an attack on these symbols of the Soviet.

Stampie, anxious for my safety, was trying to get a passage through this sudden mêlée, which appeared to have come from nowhere. They made way for the car, with no signs of animosity towards us, and renewed their stone-throwing and rude epithets.

A British officer who was on duty near the memorial was trying in vain to disperse the mob.

"Better get out while you can," he shouted to me. "They may open fire at any minute."

We were surprised at the Russians' patience in face of these taunts, but at a renewed volley of stones they made ready to open fire on the crowd, and shouted a warning. Another British officer went up and persuaded them to hold their fire while the police dealt with the angry crowd.

We did not know who the British officer was, but he behaved with such tact and patience that not a shot was fired. We remembered this later when the Soviet radio was blaring forth complaints that the British Police and Military did nothing to help the sentries or to disperse the crowds.

It was an exciting but an unpleasant experience. I had never seen a Berlin crowd in such a mood. We were becoming so accustomed to seeing them docile and even servile that we had forgotten that they could fight. It was not so long since the Battle of Berlin and they had many old scores to settle without this added blockade. Strange, though, that I felt no fear in the mob, whereas when once caught in a similar French crowd in Paris, I had been terrified. These were far more like our own crowds at home.

That evening, which was September the 9th, Stampie was witness of a much uglier incident.

He and Max had gone to attend the big meeting of the Social Democrats and Liberal Democrats, which was being held by permission of the Allies in front of the ruined Reichstag in the Platz der Republik. The Meeting was being held as a protest against the Soviet blockade, and to demonstrate the determination of the Berliners to continue the fight for a free Berlin. There were over 250,000 people present, including thousands from the East sector who had come through the Tor for the meeting.

They were addressed by Professor Ernst Reuter, their Burgomaster, and by various Trade Union leaders, and the whole proceedings were perfectly orderly, declared Stampie and Max. Max was interested in the speakers, and had gone purposely to hear them. The enthusiasm of this huge crowd seems to have been so overwhelming that they did not disperse after the meeting was finished. It was, after all, the first large gathering held in Berlin since the Occupation had banned all such meetings.

Over the Brandenburger Tor flew, as always, the Red flag, marking the beginning of the Soviet sector. It had flown there unmolested during the meeting, but now a boy, excited, and egged on by the crowd, climbed the Tor, and tearing down the flag threw it over into the British side of the gateway, where an infuriated crowd tore it to shreds. Stampie, who from a distance on a pile of ruined cement blocks had been watching, missed Max from his side, and was stupefied at seeing him the centre of the mêlée fighting for a piece of the flag. His clothing was torn, his face cut and bruised, and his hair in a wild state, as he triumphantly held a piece aloft. His face was flushed and his eyes brilliant. He looked so elated and mad that Stampie was astounded. Here was a Max he had never seen before.

"Come here, you bloody fool; you don't want to get mixed up in this—you'll lose your job in the Control Commission!" Stampie shouted above the roar of the mob as he forced his way into the fray and dragged Max out.

He remembered Fritz, and the trouble he had got into from just such a crowd as this one, and at exactly the same place. He was thinking of Frau Altmann and of how she idolized Max.

"Otherwise," he told me, "I'd have left the silly fool to get knocked about and probably arrested. As it was, there wasn't a breath left in my body when I got that bastard clear."

Having recovered his breath, he had shaken Max as one does a dog, affectionately but firmly. Max had come to his senses, apologized sheepishly, and thanked Stampie. He seemed to be in a dream, said Stampie, and had no idea why he had done it.

"I don't know what came over me," he had explained, "but when I saw that flag coming down I just had to have a piece."

"You'd better put it away quick," Stampie had advised.

Shots were being fired and the Russians, infuriated at the insult to their flag, had opened fire in the Pariser Platz and were driving jeeps ruthlessly into the crowds, while at the same time others advanced at the ready with their tommy guns, down the Friedrich Ebertstrasse into the Charlottenburg Chaussée. A British Police Major had a tough job to persuade them to withdraw into their own sector, but eventually he did, and the mob was dispersed with difficulty by the British and German police. Thirty people were badly injured, and one boy died. Most of the injuries were from gunshots, although others were caused by trampling in the crowds.

"I wouldn't have missed it for anything," declared Stampie, after giving me a graphic description. "It was as good as a football match when that flag came fluttering down."

Max had handed over the piece of flag to him, and he was going to have it framed with a brief account of the affair, he told me.

The unfortunate scapegoats chosen by the Russians for this incident were four youths all under twenty, and one man of forty. They were tried in camera by a Soviet court, and sentenced to twenty-five years' hard labour. The savagery of these sentences caused a wave of violent indignation, and even the East Zone papers, the mouthpieces of the Soviet propaganda, criticized them. The fury of the people was so great that the sentences were later somewhat reduced. Matters were made worse by the letter of protest about this incident which General Kotikov sent to General Herbert, in which the Russian General described himself as "Military Commander of the City of Berlin" and addressed General Herbert as merely "Commander of the British Garrison." The British thought this a piece of arrant impudence, but at the same time it amused them. The

Germans could not understand how we could put up with such an affront, let alone be amused by it.

"You ought to demand an apology. It's an insult to your General!" declared Max, waving a paper with a full account of it at me. He and his fellow-workers in the Control Commission had apparently been discussing it animatedly all day. He gave me some of their comments.

"How can you put up with it?" asked Karl. He was, after all, an ex-regular army officer and understood military etiquette. "It's shocking."

"I can see the funny side too," agreed Dr von R. when he asked me what we thought about it. "But their impudence is staggering." Now that Frau von R. was dead, he was living alone out at Gatow. He had got his de-nazification through, but now there were no jobs in Berlin because almost all the Control Commission was moving out into the Zone. I said that probably he would soon be able to practise again as a lawyer. He thought so too, especially now that the new currency meant that banking would start up again, and with it all kinds of legal problems. He looked tired and much older. It had taken all the reichsmarks he could raise to get his de-nazification through. I wondered what he was managing to live on—probably the potatoes which he grew in his large garden and the apples on his trees in the orchard. He showed me some tobacco plants he was growing.

The dog looked melancholy; Dr von R. said that he missed his mistress, by whose bedside he had always kept watch.

"She often talked about you," Dr. von R. said, "and hated me getting my de-nazification through. She died loyal to the Party."

I asked if she had thought it would revive.

"She was sure of it," said Dr von R. "She said that there was plenty of spirit left in the people still, and that they would throw off their yoke and revive Nazism again."

"And you?" I asked.

He shook his head smilingly. "I can't tell what the future will bring," he said, "but it has no attraction for me any more. I'm an old man now, and I want only peace."

That was what all the Berliners wanted, I thought—peace. They were sick of being fought over and quarrelled over and wrangled over, but as Frau Altmann said quaintly to me, "even *that* one gets used to—as with everything."

Stampie told me how furious the Germans were about the Kotikov-Herbert affair.

"It's damn funny. Think of all those old blimps in the War Office reading that," he chuckled.

I said that the Germans couldn't understand how we could think it funny.

"They can't understand how we thought William Joyce funny and named him Lord Haw-Haw," laughed Stampie. "They've got a funny sense of humour themselves."

"Don't forget that we used to think Hitler funny," I reminded him, "until he marched into countries just a little too near to Britain—and then it wasn't so funny."

"Too right," agreed Stampie, who had a new Australian friend and was picking up some of his expressions.

The trials of the Field-Marshals were now on, and the names of Falkenhorst, Kesselring, List and Milch were being tossed about in violent discussions as to whether or not they were war criminals. The Germans to whom I spoke about it were definite that they were not war criminals, but merely good patriots, obeying the orders from the head of their country. They were indignant that after all this time these men should be brought to trial at all.

"Why didn't you shoot them in the first place?" they said. "They are Military, and have the right to be shot if they are sentenced."

The horrors of the concentration camps at Dachau, Belsen, Buchenwald, Ravensbruck and Mauthausen were being floodlit again with the trials of those responsible for the wholesale murder of the millions of wretched inmates there. On this subject the Germans were silent. They did not want to discuss it.

Berlin was especially proud of its cultural life. It could not have been pleasant to have to admit that the perpetrators of the revolting and horrifying crimes against humanity were—

many of them—of the so-called "cultured" world. The doctors whom I knew at the various hospitals were following the trials of the prison camp medical attendants with growing incredulity and horror. They did not deny the facts. They had not known, they said. But what could they have done if they had known? One was powerless.

"They all knew," insisted Frau Pfeiffer and Frau Altmann, who had reason to know themselves. "Everyone knew that these places existed because one was threatened with them, but just how appalling was the cruelty there many possibly did not know."

The account of the notorious Frau Ilse Koch had a morbid attraction for Stampie. He couldn't get over it as he pored over a photograph of her in a newspaper.

"She ought to be skinned alive and then made to look at lampshades made from her own skin; perhaps she'd enjoy that a bit less than she did those she had made from those poor devils in the camp. God! It makes one sick to think of it. And here we are, saving all these little German kids so that they'll grow up and do the same."

Stampie was indignant when he heard that Frau Ilse Koch was not to be skinned alive or even hanged. She was merely sentenced to penal servitude. Her husband had already been executed after his trial at Nuremburg.

VI

FRAU ALTMANN and Max were alone now in the ruined house. It was terribly quiet and strange without Ursula, Frau Altmann said. She missed her far more than she had thought she could. When Ursula was around there were always life and movement, arguments and often quarrels, but she was vitally alive, and it was this quality which was her great attraction. Her mother had resented it, because it drew attention to the girl, but she missed it now.

I learned a good deal more about Frau Altmann herself now that she was alone so much. She had told me very little about herself—she was not the sort of woman who cared to speak about her own personal life or experiences. She would talk of Kurt, of Fritz, of Oskar and of Ursula—anyone except herself.

I knew that she had learned her almost perfect English in England where she had taken a course at Oxford, and that she knew our country fairly well. It was with surprise that I learned from her that she had been engaged to a young undergraduate at Oxford, and that she had not married Oskar until ten years after her fiancé's death.

One day when she had quoted some verses of Rupert Brooke to me and I had commented on her amazing knowledge of English poetry she had said:

"Edward used to read poetry to me when we were engaged—not Rupert Brooke, of course—Edward died long before the First World War—but Keats and Shelley and Browning. He loved them, and I have always loved your poetry. It was a great pleasure to me when I found that Kurt wanted to go to Oxford and take a course in English. Had it not been for the war he would have gone." Kurt had gone to Russia instead—to that terrible Eastern Front from which millions of Germans had never returned. Almost every family we knew had a member missing in Russia.

"It was all so very long ago," she went on, smiling, "when we were both at Oxford and my father was stationed in London in the Embassy. He and Edward used to go climbing in your lovely Lake District, and it was there that Edward lost his life in trying to save a child who had fallen in one of the lakes—he was drowned—a week before we were to have been married."

From an album she took a fading photograph. "This was Edward," she said.

There was nothing in the serious young face to indicate what kind of young man Edward had been. He looked scared of the camera and stood in a slightly ridiculous pose before the entrance to a photographer's arbour, tall and athletic in spite of the clothes of the period.

"He loved poetry," sighed Frau Altmann. "And he loved his country as Rupert Brooke did."

If that were so, at least she had been spared the horror of a marriage endangered by war between their two countries. I had seen so much suffering in this last war in families of mixed marriages torn asunder because of different nationality.

"It is years since I spoke of him," she mused, putting the photograph carefully away, "but it seems only yesterday that we used to go climbing with Father."

She must have been very much in love with Edward, for she had not married Oskar until ten years later, although he had wooed her for several years.

"But you were happy in your marriage?" I asked.

"Wonderfully happy," she said. "Oskar was a good man and an unselfish one. We had many good years and many bad together—the bad ones were in the two terrible wars of course—and all the worries and joys of the children. And that is how it should be—everything shared—joy and sorrow alike."

She shut the album, putting the little sprig of rosemary back with it.

"When one gets older it is lovely to look back into the past, and the strange thing is that the past becomes nearer than the future," she said. "The children cannot understand that. Ursula and Lilli never thought that I could understand love. To them I was an old woman, and it is true that Fritz and Lilli were born when I was well over forty—Kurt is ten years older than Fritz, you know—but those days by the lakes in England seem nearer to me now than the years of the terrible bombing here."

She asked me about London during the war and we compared some of our experiences.

I remembered how pleased Frau von R. had been when she had heard that our home had been completely destroyed by the Luftwaffe, and that we had been buried in it.

"So," she had said with satisfaction, "you know what bombing is like." And when I had retorted that the Luftwaffe had done its best to show us, she had said coldly, "Our bombing of London was nothing to the Allies' inexcusable attacks on Berlin."

Frau Altmann had looked at the photographs of the ruins of our home and marvelled that we had ever come out of it alive. When I told her that all our neighbours had been killed but that we had been spared, she said with conviction, "God saved you for His own good purpose—and your husband and your unborn son too—none of these things are accidental, they are all part of God's plan."

I never ceased to marvel that after all she had suffered she still had an unshaken faith in God.

Max was working very hard trying to finish his engineering exams so that he could take his degree. He had little free time, and although he was at home most evenings studying, Frau Altmann was lonely; I could tell that by the great welcome she always gave me on arrival. She was losing her pupils, as they were being moved out of Berlin. The air-lift was feeding 250,000 people, and every mouth able to find its food in the Zone helped. The Allies were moving out at great speed now, and this not only meant the loss of work and personal ties and help for many Germans, but it also brought increased fear that soon Berlin would be left to its fate.

"One cannot expect this wonderful *Luftbrücke* to continue indefinitely," said Frau Altmann. "It is costing millions, and your brave airmen are losing their lives feeding us. What will be the end of it all?"

The hundredth day of the air-lift had passed. On this day the United States air-lift had brought in the record load of 1,104 tons of food, and the R.A.F. ran it close with over 1,000 tons.

Goods were being flown out too, and thus trade with the outer world was made possible. We got all the details from Stampie, who was "in the know." The planes, he told me, flew in with food and coal and other necessities, and went out laden with manufactured goods made in Berlin and bought by the West.

"And they're going to fly all the sick and undernourished kids out before it gets too cold," he told us. "They'll get a better chance where there's more food and more warmth."

He was helping Max with various experiments he had to make, and with all kinds of problems connected with his studies. A small engineering school was now open, and although the fees were high Max was managing to pay them while he was working for the British. His one fear was that the branch where he worked would soon be moving out too. They were going as soon as a place in the Zone could be found. It was by no means easy to fit all these governmental departments into an overcrowded and underhoused Zone. The Control Commission officials were grumbling at the less luxurious and spacious accommodation they had to be content with in the Zone.

"Makes you mad when you think of old Sokolovsky sitting there laughing his head off to think of all the trouble he's causing us," said Stampie. "And the joke is, that he can do it again just whenever he feels like it. That autobahn is just a mouse-run and he's the cat sitting pretty waiting to spring."

I asked how his cat, Lenin, was. Apparently he was fine. Now that he drove a lorry the cat could accompany him everywhere. The Boss in the cloak-and-dagger set-up had objected to Lenin's presence in the car.

"Probably because his name was Lenin," said Stampie with a grin. "Got no sense of humour, these chaps haven't."

Lenin now accompanied his master everywhere, and scraps of food were saved for him at many places. He was getting quite fat and was very clever.

"Understands everything I say to him," declared his master.

He sensed as I did that Frau Altmann was lonely, and with her pupils all leaving she was depressed and apprehensive of the future, although she gave no sign that she worried. I asked her if she was willing to help me with the distribution of some of the parcels, and if she would take on the weekly delivers, such as that for the child Krista, who depended on these vitamins and cod liver oil, etc. for their progress. She was delighted, and I arranged for her to do the families near her, as there was almost no transport and she looked too frail to walk far. Petrol had to be flown in, and its use was much curtailed. Coal had to be flown in too, so there were few railway and tram services. Frau Altmann was undaunted by all this; she had always been a great walker, and, like me, she loved it. I also arranged for her to get some teaching from one of the British schools, although this was rather far away for her.

Ursula had written, not much but just to say that all was well and that she would write a long letter soon. She had also written to me.

"The people are overwhelming with their welcome and kindness," she had written, "and I wonder if they really mean it. Why should they show so much kindness to a German girl—a former enemy—when they would surely have rather their son had married an American girl?"

I did not show this to her mother. Frau Altmann was the sort of woman who accepted a kindness on its face value and treasured it. She would have been upset at this rather suspicious and questioning attitude of her daughter.

I did not tell her either that a letter had come from my friends in Leipzig, enclosing the announcement of a meeting of the Free German Youth Movement. There was a photograph of one of the leaders who was to speak at it. No comment was made on the cutting in the letter, but the reason for its inclusion was obvious. The man in the photograph had a small moustache, but I was positive that it was Fritz. He had an unusual face, the drawing of the cheekbones being particularly interesting. The eyes too were rather like Ursula's, set at a slight slant and sloping up at the corners. One could not be mistaken over these things. I debated for some time whether or not to show it to her, and decided against it, for the flag under which he stood in the photograph was a similar one to the ill-fated red flag which had caused the Brandenburger Tor incident.

When Frau Altmann had been shown Stampie's piece in an elaborate frame she had said sharply that she was surprised that he should waste money on framing such an infamous thing, and that any political party which was against the Church was doomed to extinction—as the Nazi Party had been.

"God," she said, "is patient, but there are certain things which He cannot overlook, and one of them is surely the deliberate turning away of His people from the Church."

So stern and emphatic had been her voice that Stampie and Max had been silent, and the framed piece of material had been thrust back into Stampie's pocket.

How then could I show her this photograph of her be-loved youngest born, not only standing under it but from his enthusiastic expression advocating adherence to it?

SPRING

1949

IT WAS NOT until March that Frau Altmann became really ill. She must have struggled for months with pain before she finally went to her doctor. She had never been a coward, and there was no hiding the truth from her now. She had cancer of the lungs and she was too weak for an operation. Max, who was still with her, had written to me several times that she was not well, but although she was in constant touch with me she had never mentioned that she was ill. I had seen her just before Christmas and had been shocked at her thinness and transparent look. She had insisted that she was perfectly well.

We were living in Westphalia now, my husband's branch having been transferred from Berlin, but I went back there as often as possible. One could get out of Berlin easily enough in the empty planes which had brought in the food. Getting a seat in a plane to go there was not so easy. Official visits came first and others had to be wangled. The welfare parcels which were now being sent direct to me in Westphalia were taken on by the air-lift, and Dr Annemarie and Frau Altmann dealt with them at the other end. We used to take them out to the airport at Bückeburg and hand them to the pilots. Whenever they had space they took them and, what is more, they delivered them personally or found a colleague to do so. They never refused a parcel, and not one was lost or mislaid. John used to love watching the food being loaded from the lorries into the great fleet of waiting planes.

The air-lift had already begun transporting delicate and undernourished children and their mothers or escorts out of the city before winter set in. They also took a number of very ill patients who could not receive the treatment they needed in Berlin owing to the shortage of supplies. Between September and February the R.A.F. flew 12,333 of these children without mishap out of Berlin, and almost a thousand mothers and escorts.

The Berliners were having a thin time, as their letters told me.

It was a shock when I got a letter from Max in March telling me that Frau Altmann was very ill and in hospital. I wrote to the hospital, which was one I knew well. The professor in charge of her case replied at once, telling me that there was no hope whatsoever for her in Berlin, and he proposed to have her flown out to some hospital in the Zone where there would be facilities for radium and x-ray treatment. He suggested that she came to Hanover or Minden so that she would be near me. Her husband had been an old friend of his, and he would get in touch with the professors at whatever hospital would take her.

A week later she was flown out to Bückeburg and an ambulance from the hospital met her. She had never flown in her life, and in spite of her pain and weakness she had enjoyed the experience, and insisted on thanking the pilot who came round to see how the old lady had stood her first flight. He was astonished at her perfect English, and charmed with her.

"She's a game one," he said. "Is she very ill?" I told him what was wrong. He asked me which hospital she was going to. When she woke next day from the heavy drug they had given her, she found a mass of flowers by her bedside from this young pilot. Some of these young lads were wonderfully good to the children they transported, and saved all their chocolate and sweet rations to hand round on the trips. Nothing was too much trouble for them. They would take messages, telephone people, post parcels on arrival or deliver them if they could. They were beyond praise.

Germans build their hospitals, whenever possible, high on a hill away from the dust and dirt of the town, so that the patients shall not only get fresher air, but also a lovely view. They build them with terraces so that the patients can lie out and have something beautiful to look at.

The hospital where Frau Altmann now lay was high on a hill above the Weser. She was calm and in no way disturbed by the other patients round her. Indeed she liked their company. She begged me not to tell Ursula how ill she was. Ursula was expecting a baby in July and must not be worried. She was happy in her new home and her relatives were wonderfully kind, she said.

Frau Altmann talked a great deal about the baby.

"My first grandchild," she said. "How Pappi would have loved to see Ursula's child!" If it was a boy it was to be called Francis Joseph—Francis after Joe's father—and if it was a girl it would be named Liliane after Lilli.

"Is she really happy, do you think?" I asked her.

She said thoughtfully, "I think she is as happy as she deserves to be."

The professor told me that Frau Altmann could not stand an operation. Her heart, he said, was in a very dangerous state, and the cancer in both lungs was far advanced. Treatment such as they could give with the limited means at their disposal was negligible.

"We are far behind in medicine," he explained to me. "We have been prevented from attending the international medical conferences for years now, and we don't understand the use of all the wonderful new drugs, even if we could get them."

I told him I could get almost anything he needed for Frau Altmann from British or American doctor friends.

He patted me on the shoulder and said sadly: "The one thing she needs, no one can give her."

I asked him if she would have much pain. He said, "I shall not let her suffer more than she can bear—but I think she is the kind who will not let us know how much she is suffering."

He was right. Whenever I asked Frau Altmann how she was, she invariably replied that she was very well and never said that she was in pain, but each time I saw her the havoc in her face told its own story.

We used to talk about the children, for that she loved best. All about Kurt when he was a little boy, about how wilful and naughty Ursula always was, how sweet and biddable was Lilli. She showed me photographs of them all; they were the only things she had brought with her beyond her few toilet necessities. I think she knew when she set out on that first air journey that she would never come back, and would never need her clothes again.

Max wrote regularly with all the news he could find. He had done as she wished and taken a lodger to share his room to make it cheaper for him. Her room was all ready for when she returned. He was digging the garden and planting potatoes for her. His friend was helping. They had cleared away mounds of rubble now, and were clearing the earth of stones. The primroses were out and the lilac in bud. It was already quite hot in Berlin. They were getting a new kind of dehydrated potato flown in; it was called "Pom" and tasted like warm flannel. Potatoes took up too much space, and dehydrated ones in packets were simpler. "But," he wrote, "what wouldn't we give for a good solid potato! That is why I am determined to grow them for you in case the air-lift is still on next year."

Hermann and his wife wrote too. They gave lurid details of their hardships, and it upset Frau Altmann when her trays of food came in.

"If only I could send some of this to Luise and Hermann," she would sigh.

I felt sure that Hermann was not doing too badly. Stampie would see to that. He had come out twice to see us on trips which one of his R.A.F. friends had wangled for him.

"Not but what I didn't earn it, mind you," he said. "I did five hours' loading at each end." He had achieved his ambition at last, and was on air-lift duties driving a food lorry.

"Bit of all right here," he had exclaimed when he had explored our new home and examined the dogs and John carefully. "But you'll soon be back in Berlin. Old Joe Stalin is getting sick of the fuss over this air-lift—you'll see."

I asked him about Hermann and Luise.

"They're no worse off than anyone else," he assured me, "but I'm going scrounging round for my Mess while I'm here. We could do with a meal that isn't out of a packet."

The farmers, he said, would give them anything in exchange for coffee, which they still could not get. He and his R.A.F. friend were going to make the rounds that evening before returning to Berlin, and hoped to take back some "solid" food.

Apparently he was very successful, for the next letter from Luise said that they had had a wonderful feast after Mr Stamp's visit to the West. They had actually had sausage and real eggs, "not the powder which tasted of fish."

Frau Altmann was interested in every one of my refugee families. She remembered their names, their children and their ailments, and asked for the latest news each time I saw her. She was so alert mentally that it was difficult to believe she was dying. But the professor told me that she was getting weaker and weaker.

One lovely afternoon in May when I reached the hospital I found that she had been moved out of the ward into a small private annexe. There were large windows and a wonderful view over the hills down to the river. Her bed was near the window and had been raised up high so that she could look out.

"Isn't it lovely?" she asked me. "I believe this is the first class here."

It was. German hospitals have three classes according to the amount their patients can pay. Max, Stampie and I were paying for Frau Altmann. This hospital was an expensive one, and I asked the sister about the cost of this small private annexe.

"Don't worry," she said. "Frau Altmann has been put here by the professor's special orders. There will not be any extra charge for Frau Altmann. We all admire her great courage, and the professor realizes what you are doing for the refugees here."

There was a wonderful view from her windows and I took my sketching things, and sitting there would work, and at the same time tell her about everything I could see. She was getting too weak now to remain up on her pillows for long. She loved to watch me, and took an intense interest in the sketches and in all that went on down in the valley.

She could hear the birds and the cows, and from the hospital gardens the scent of lilac and syringa came through her open windows.

"It is so lovely here. How lucky I am to be in the country at such a time of year. The world is so beautiful, only the people in it are so ugly and wicked," she would sigh.

From the sketches I was making a landscape now, and this she watched enthralled.

"You must be one of the happiest of women," she said. "You can lose yourself so completely in your work—nothing else matters when you are painting, does it?"

I said, yes, that it was a wonderful escape, but one seldom achieved what one wanted, that it had its drawbacks if one were married and a mother.

"You wouldn't be complete without them, and your work would lack some quality," she insisted.

I wondered. From some of the extraordinary daubs now being hung in the exhibitions, it would not have mattered whether the artists were never born, to say nothing of being complete.

One afternoon when the painting was almost finished and the professor had been talking to us, she said, "What can I do to repay him for all his goodness to me? He is wonderful, and he knows that I have no money."

I said I would paint his portrait if he liked. He was a fine-looking old man and would make a very interesting portrait. She was delighted, but said that it would be me doing something for him and not her.

"It's all the same," I told her. "I will get the pleasure of a good sitter—for all doctors are good sitters—and he will get the portrait, and you will be happy, *nicht wahr*?"

We arranged it and the professor began the sittings at once.

One day she asked me if I had ever heard anything of Fritz. We had been talking about John and she had been recounting some anecdotes of Fritz when he was a child. She asked the question out of the blue, and I was taken unawares and said yes, that I knew where he was. She listened in silence while I told her about the photograph.

"I'd like to see it, please," she said quietly.

I showed it to her.

"Yes, it's Fritz," she said at length. "Promise me that if you ever see him you will give him a message from me."

It seemed highly unlikely that Fritz's path and mine would ever cross again and I gave the promise.

"Tell him," she said slowly, "this: No matter what flag he marches under or fights for—whether it be the swastika, the hammer and sickle, or any other—when death comes to him—as it comes to us all—he will need only the Cross. Tell him to heed what his mother says, because she knows."

It was so lovely in the Weser valley that May. The beauty of the blossoming orchards and the great hills covered in a new and tender wash of green was incredible after the grey ruins of Berlin. The sides of the hills were carpeted with *Windblumen*, or anemones, and blue violets made lovely splashes of colour among the green and white. The lilies-of-the-valley would soon be out; they grew in great profusion on the shady sides of the hills. Lotte and I were watching for them; we had promised the first bunch to Frau Altmann, who had gathered them on these very hills as a girl.

One afternoon, it was the 12th of May, we climbed Great Wilhelm, the highest hill of all those round us, and we found the lilies in full bloom. They were growing in profusion and we gathered them in great bunches.

When we got home there was a telephone message from the hospital. Frau Altmann was worse.

She was lying there looking out of the windows when I reached the hospital. Her face, which had become very ethereal, now had a luminousness which did not come only from the light. It had been a glorious day, and the sun, a ball of flame, was just beginning to sink a little behind the range of hills. Its light flooded the river below, and she was watching it.

The sister brought tea, and beckoned me outside.

"I am glad you have come," she whispered. "She is very weak and has been rambling a little. She is having a lot of drugs now."

Frau Altmann drank some tea, and pushed her face into the sweet-scented flowers. I told her how they lay in a great carpet up on the hills.

"It is strange," she said with a very sweet smile, "that it is you who are here with me now. Do you remember when you first saw me? I remember it so well—that heavy cart and all those things falling in the road—how kind you were—like an angel. I would like to thank you for everything—but between us no words of thanks are necessary, we understand each other, *nicht wahr?* Gott wird Dich belohnen."

I could not speak, my throat ached so much. This woman meant a great deal to me. She stood for something rapidly disappearing—something precious.

"Give me your hands," she said, releasing the flowers suddenly, her face twisting with pain, "and tell me what you see from the window." She had often asked me to do this.

I wanted to call sister. Her hands were so cold, and her face so terribly pale, but she begged me not to.

"Tell me what you can see from the window," she said again, "for I am too weak to raise myself now—I feel sleepy."

I said: "The river is turning from gold to red as the sun sinks—it is like a sheet of flame. The hills are dark and rugged against this fiery background. A flight of duck are coming home . . ."

"It is good that they are coming home," she said, her voice not much more than a whisper, "for it is surely getting very dark now."

Her head fell back suddenly, and I called loudly for sister, who came running in. She removed my hands very gently from Frau Altmann's and rang the bell. A nurse came running in.

"Ask the Herr Professor to come immediately," she said sharply.

When he came he took me away.

"She went easily, thank God," he said. "It could have been agony for her."

The sister was putting the lilies in her hands as we left the sun-filled room.

At one minute past midnight, on May 13th, 1949, the blockade of Berlin was lifted. Lotte, who had been listening to the radio in her room, came running down to me in her dressing gown.

"It's over," she cried. There were tears in her eyes. "It's over."

British and American lorries and military vehicles crossed the zonal frontier that night from Helmstedt and proceeded without mishap to Berlin. A few days later the first Allied trains ran from Bielefeld and Frankfort, without interference, to Berlin. The blockade was really over.

After Frau Altmann's death Max was at a loss what to do about the house. With Ursula so far away, and Fritz where he could not be got at, there were only Hermann and his wife. Max himself was only a second cousin, but Frau Altmann had loved him as a son, and I had noticed the charming way he had looked after her and the deference he invariably showed her. It was touching to see the way this tall well-built man would take her out, treating her as if she were a piece of valuable china which might break at any moment. He knew only too well that her days were numbered and had treasured them. She had told me how good he had been to her, how nothing was too much trouble for him to do for her when she was first too ill to do things for herself.

"He will make a wonderful husband," she had sighed; "not like most of our men, who will not do anything at all."

"That is partly the fault of the German women," I said. "You do not like your men to help in the house, you like to wait on them. Max has seen the British way in which some, at least, of the menfolk help a great deal."

He had written constantly to her while she was in the hospital, but the end came so suddenly that it had not been possible to summon him. He had come to the funeral.

She had asked, to my great surprise, to be buried in the churchyard under the great hill.

"How silly I was to make all that fuss about Pappi," she had said. "I know now that death doesn't matter at all—it is but a passing to a new life and the means of getting there, and the means of disposal of the body can have no possible influence on the soul. You've always thought that, haven't you?"

I said, "I wish I had your faith."

"You must suffer and suffer—and you will discover that there is no other answer than God," she replied simply.

"If, later on, Ursula or the boys wish to put me beside Pappi and Lilli, that is their affair. I am content to lie up there under the great hill which I have loved looking at."

We buried her there. She lay between an old man from East Prussia and a little child from Breslau. The professor had done his best for them too.

I told Max about this conversation. He was cynical and sceptical.

"Surely you don't believe in all that stuff about the soul," he scoffed. "You are an intelligent woman. But she belonged to the old school and if it gave her comfort I am glad."

"You would be better for a faith like hers," I said, "as we all would."

"Perhaps I have it," he said surprisingly, "but not for Christianity."

We were sitting in the lovely May sunshine with the pastor, who was a great friend of ours, and who had visited Frau Altmann frequently. He had been in a Russian prison camp, and she had listened eagerly to all he could tell her. She had thirsted for news of her son Kurt, and had questioned him in vain. All around us lay the most exquisite wide landscape. Our house in the valley had a wonderful view across the Weser.

"You are seeing a lot of misery and many deaths," said the pastor to me, "but you also see all this"—throwing out his arms in the direction of the landscape—"and that is surely a compensation of the Creator."

Many of my refugees from the East Zone had died that winter, and we were trying to get the local authorities to grant the survivors the right to accommodation in place of the miserable huts and caves in which they now lived like animals.

"Why do you do it? Why don't you just let them die?" asked Max angrily. "What's it got to do with you? Death is easy—it's much more difficult to go on living in this mess here."

"Why did you do all you could for Frau Altmann?" I asked him.

"Tante Maria was different—besides she was a relative, and I loved her, but these wretched people are not only strangers to you, but they are still enemies—as I am. You British have not yet made peace with us. Isn't that true?"

He was angry and miserable. I asked him what he intended to do now. He didn't know. His uncle wanted him to finish his examinations and then come to him in Bavaria.

"And will you go?" I asked. The uncle was obviously a man of substance; he had sent money for the funeral, and money several times for Frau Altmann. He had sent it to me through American friends, Bavaria being in the U.S. Zone.

"I shall go as soon as the exam is over and the house is arranged. Ursula will have to say what she wishes done about it."

"Have you written to her?" I asked him.

"I got the lawyers to write," he said stiffly.

"Her baby is due very soon now," I said. "Otherwise she would come over, I think."

"A baby?" he said in surprise. "Ursula is going to have a baby? How very funny!" And he began to laugh in such a bitter way that I checked him angrily.

Frau Altmann hadn't told him. She had seen much more than one would have thought. Perhaps the lesson of her blindness over Lilli had taught her something. She had known that he loved Ursula.

I said to him: "Go and talk to some of the young farmers round here. You will find them very interesting. They are close to the earth and have no illusions about anything."

"It is said that many of them are still interested in the Nazi Party, and that there is of revivalist movement in these parts," observed the pastor.

"So I gather from my son, who has the run of the farms," I said. "The farmers are very good to him and he is having a wonderful life here, but they do not realise how much German he understands. He takes in a great deal, and repeats it all to me."

"And do you mix much with them?" asked Max.

I told him I was making friends rapidly with several of the wives of the big farmers round us. He was interested, and before he returned to Berlin I sent him to visit some of the ones I knew.

AUTUMN

1949

It was October 1949, and Berlin was in a ferment of excitement over the huge demonstration planned by the Soviet to celebrate the election of Wilhelm Pieck as President of their newly formed German Democratic Party.

The West, expecting ugly incidents again, had rushed large drafts of police to Berlin. The Military were ready. Leave to Berlin had not been encouraged. Anything might happen. The Berliners were tense and furious about the whole thing.

Berlin had changed but little outwardly, yet underneath there was a great difference in the whole feeling and set-up. Since the end of the blockade there had been plenty of smaller troubles: the railway strike, which had left the poor citizens without transport again for six weeks; the constant hopes through the three-Power meetings with Stalin of a settlement of some kind of way of life for Berlin—and their death through the further demands of Molotov, in a fresh deadlock. It seemed as if the very air of Berlin was uneasy and cast some antagonistic spell over all negotiations, for the talks which had seemed so hopeful in London had come to grief as soon as they moved to Berlin.

The West was beginning to get on its feet again; we could see that all round us. There was a new feeling. No longer was the German to be treated as an outcast. We were no longer forbidden to be friends with them—on the contrary, it was now being encouraged.

"We have been very naughty boys," said a farmer to me with a sly grin, "and now we have worn sackcloth and ashes Mother Britain is patting us on the head and saying: 'Now, now, we can't forget what you have done, but we can forget it conveniently enough for you to help us against the Russians, with whom we are no longer so friendly as we were.'"

This was apparent in the attitude of the women with whom we were now asked to try and make friends. It was too late. They had wanted to be friends as soon as we came. They had been repulsed. The wife of a very prominent German politician expressed herself to me on the subject after we had been listening to a talk on the British and Germans getting together now and being friends.

"You British are very sporting-minded," she said. "After a fight you shake hands publicly—if it is football, tennis or boxing—but now after this fight, what happened? You came as conquerors. Good. We expected that. We had earned it ourselves. But you have put up too many degrading notices, too many 'Germans Keep Out' everywhere, for it to be easy for us to fall in with your desire for friendship now. Had you held out your hand when you first came we would have taken it gladly." This lady was a Hanoverian, and bitterly resented our first attitude. She said: "Your Royal Family came from here, you have our coat of arms. You should at least have treated us Hanoverians differently—we even fought for your kings in the past."

The Berliner was different. Through privations under the Russians and the joint endurance with the British of the blockade, they had formed a far better understanding of our actions. They had shared everything. They were grateful to us, and, what is more, they depended on us for their very existence as a free city.

Max had been astonished at the different feeling in the West, just as I had been. In the West they didn't care at all about Berlin.

"But it's your capital," I would say. "You must care—it stands for freedom."

"You are making a new capital," they replied, "further away from the Russians. Why all this fuss, why don't you let the Russians have Berlin? This air-lift is still costing us taxes—why should we pay for the Berliners?"

"I am very glad to have gone out, if only to see the difference," said Max when I met him that autumn in Berlin. "Here we live in a private world, on our island, and we are apt to forget how small we are."

He had finished his examinations successfully, and was going to Munich to be near his uncle. Hermann and his wife were living in the Altmann house and Max was with them, paying his share.

"But I can't stand it," he told me. "Hermann is impossible. He is always drinking and I can't get on with him. I try to protect Tante Luise as much as I can. I am strong and can knock Hermann out when he gets tiresome."

I asked where Hermann got the drink.

"He has bartered all the furniture and silver now. They were glad to come and live here, for their own flat was practically empty, but I see that he doesn't start that little game with Tante Maria's things in this house."

"And what will happen when you are gone?" I asked.

Max said that he would not be able to help then, but he intended to put the fear of God into Hermann before he went, and Stampie had promised to keep an eye on them.

"He will; he is devoted to Hermann," I said.

We were going that evening to the Unter den Linden to see the celebrations for the new Democratic Party. I wanted to see this new Free German Youth movement, about which I had heard a great deal from Lotte, whose sister's children in the East Zone were always talking of it. They were still young, but Barbel, John's friend, and the eldest of them, would soon be obliged to join. These girls and boys were to form a huge procession, and later have a torchlight parade in honour of Herr Pieck, and they had come from all over the East Zone to Berlin for this great day.

There was no difficulty in seeing the procession. The Soviet authorities wanted everyone to see it—especially the West. All factory workers had been given a holiday to see the demonstration, and the place was crowded. It was raining a little, but it was not enough to damp the ardour of the young people in the parade. They marched with their huge pictures of Pieck and Stalin with their flags and banners, and they were fine and strong and they looked fit and happy. Useless for the Western press to say next day that they were spiritless. Impossible not to be horrified and at the same time impressed. There were so many, and they were so well drilled.

Stampie had been angry that he was not free to come with us. He had been back on normal driving duties since the airlift ended, and he did not like it. He liked lorries; he had got used to them, and he had liked the free and easy life among the R.A.F. men.

He couldn't come with us that evening because he had to take his boss to a dinner party, and he resented my going without him to look after me.

"Supposin' that Max takes it into his head to tear down another piece of flag—there'll be plenty of hammers and sickles about. What will you do if he goes off and the crowd gets rough? Tell you what—I'll try and get a pal to drive for me tonight. I can always have a headache—I'm entitled to be ill same as anyone else."

I assured him that Max would not do anything silly, and also that I could look after myself.

"Does the Boss know you are going to it?" he asked me.

I shook my head. The Boss did not.

And here we stood, Max and I, watching this enormous Rally of Youth. Column upon column of fine young people, heads up, shoulders back, chests out, banners and portraits held proudly as high as the flags. Into my mind there swept the picture of the Nuremberg Rally all those years ago. Only the colour of the uniform distinguished them from those others who marched under the Swastika. Here was the same ardour, the same proud march, the same intoxicating sense of power. I looked at the spectators: they were absolutely thrilled. I looked at Max: he was dead white, and a small muscle in his cheek twitched in his emotion. It was terrifying, and it went on and on and on—more and more of these strong young limbs moving in perfect unison, and as they marched one heard in one's mind the roll of drums and the thunder of guns and the roar of planes.

I thought of Frau Altmann's words. I had commented on the resentment of the Germans that in the British zone any kind of uniform was banned.

"It is right," she had said. "Men are fools. Give them a flag and a shirt exactly like their neighbours' and they will think they are gods."

The People's Police came next in their smart uniforms. They were armed, and military in every detail—a German Army, in spite of the Potsdam Agreement. One could understand the justice of the British Military Government's protests that these so-called Police were in reality an army trained under von Seydlitz and von Paulus.

How clever the Russians had been! While men of call-up age were unemployed and kicking their heels in our zone looking vainly for a meal ticket, the Soviet had directed their unemployed through the Labour Exchanges into this Police Force. Those who were fit and were between eighteen and thirty-five had been trained into splendid physical condition, armed, put into smart uniforms, and told:

"Now you're in the People's Police, it's up to you to keep order in the State we have founded for you."

These men were in every respect the replicas of the former SS troops, and the one hundred and fifty smartest of them— all picked men—were to be inspected by Pieck. And here he came, the man whom Fritz had admired, a little weary-looking old man standing in an open car and acknowledging the roars of the crowd, as his former bitter opponent, Hitler, had so often done. The carpenter and the house painter—but on opposite sides of the fence, or were they?

At last it was over and the young people and the workers were being addressed by their new President. They had been given full sovereignty by the generous Soviet, he told them, and there were not enough words for the thanks we owed the Soviet Union and Stalin for this generous action.

Max clutched me by the arm.

"I think I am going to be sick," he said.

"Shut up! Silence there!" hissed a man next to us. The crowd was listening with the rapt breathlessness that they had once given Hitler at the Nazi rallies. It was incredible.

Max looked really ill. Sweat was pouring from his forehead and he was dead white, with what I now realized was fury.

"It's disgusting," he muttered.

The man next to us turned on him angrily.

"Be quiet!" he snarled.

I thought we had better get out—and suddenly I saw Fritz. He was standing on a raised platform addressing some of the Youth Movement who were getting ready now for the Torch-light Procession which was to end the Rally. He wore their uniform, and two youths stood on either side of him holding great pictures of Stalin and Pieck.

"Max!" I whispered, "hold on a bit, do. Look at that fair man up there—that's Fritz!"

"Are you sure?" he hissed.

"Positive. Let's get nearer to him, *please*."

It wasn't easy. The crowd was dense and enthralled, and no one wanted to make way for us. We had to push very slowly and very carefully towards our objective. Even as we got nearer it began to break up, and progress was appallingly difficult. I hate crowds and began to feel quite ill. It was impossible to breathe; people pressed against one's chest, and I thought of a terrible incident in London when so many people had been just squeezed to death in a panic on some steps leading down to a shelter.

Max, who was huge and pushed a way for me as well as he could, was sweating himself.

"Let's give it up," he begged, above the roar of the crowd. "You'll get hurt, and I shall get into trouble."

"I'm going to deliver that message from his mother if I get trampled to death doing it," I shouted.

"All right then, lean against me and push," he yelled.

Afterwards I couldn't think what had possessed me to do such a thing. It must have been the excitement and the infectious madness of the crowd. I felt that nothing in the world mattered but my objective, and that was Fritz. I was going to tell him what his mother said somehow. We pushed and fought and did everything except bite, and suddenly we were there by the raised stand and there was Fritz standing at the head of a column of youngsters.

"Fritz!" I yelled.

He turned. He had recognized me. A flicker of something almost like pleasure, and yet more like fear, crossed his face and he turned away and gave some orders to the children.

I grabbed his arm.

"Fritz! I must speak to you—please!"

He spoke to another man in the same uniform as his, and then turned round again.

"Meet me over there," he pointed to a less crowded part of the street, "in ten minutes. I can't come with you. I'll join you there."

"Promise?" I asked.

He nodded. "I give you my word."

We struggled again. Max was as exhausted as I was, but he forced a way for me with his great bulk. When we got to the fairly clear space indicated by Fritz he mopped his face and said: "Well, well, not so bad for the moderate British. I never thought you could stand that."

"You should know by now that we are tougher than we appear," I said, sinking down on to a stone on a pile of debris. We sat there recovering our breath. What we wanted was a drink, but that was impossible. We smoked a cigarette and got cooler. Some of the uniformed children were standing about near us. We called some of them and talked to them. They came from all over the Zone. Some had come hundreds of miles for this. They were to see all the sights of Berlin— although there were not many left to see. They were tired, and some were damp from the drizzling rain which had now stopped, but they were enthusiastic and happy. They had been told not to go into the British and American sectors, although some of them had relatives there whom they wanted to visit.

"But I'm going," said one boy. "Mother said I could."

"Won't you get into trouble?" we asked.

Apparently not. They had to obey certain rules. They had been brought by their leaders who were responsible for them, and naturally they would obey them, but they had not actually been forbidden to go, only advised to stay in their own sector.

I could not see that they were very different from our girl guides and boy scouts as they stood about in little groups. It was when they were marching that they were so terrifying. I said so to Max.

"The only way to deal with these Communists is to match them with something even stronger and more ruthless. You have a saying I like in Britain: 'Set a thief to catch a thief' isn't it? Well, what's the good of fighting this with a Socialist Government? You want something more ruthless and brutal than your tolerant middle path."

"A dictatorship, in fact?"

"If necessary, yes," he said quietly.

I was about to protest when Fritz appeared. We had almost given him up. Max had been sure that he would not come, but here he was coming towards us hurriedly.

I looked at him carefully. He had grown a moustache and his hair was cut short and was almost shaved in its military neatness. He had filled out. His shoulders no longer drooped, his head was held high. His eyes were no longer hopeless, they were filled with an almost fanatical light.

"Do we shake hands?" he asked smiling. I introduced Max. They had not met since Fritz was a child.

"I can't stay long," he apologized hurriedly. "I am in charge of all those youngsters over there, and until we dismiss I am on duty. My colleague has taken over for me for half an hour; shall we go over and get a drink somewhere?"

"It's hopeless," said Max. "Have a cigarette?"

"You look well," I told him. "In fact, you look wonderfully fit. Are you happy?"

He nodded emphatically. "Very happy indeed, thank you."

I said: "Look, I came for one reason only, Fritz, to give you a message from your mother. You know she is dead?" He bowed his head.

"How?" I asked in astonishment.

"From Tante Karin," he said.

"You see them?" I asked. For there had been no word of Fritz in the letter she had written me after I had told her of her sister's death.

"Only recently—the boy, my cousin Heinz, is a member of the Youth Movement. I recognized the name although I had never seen him, and found out where they were living. They had left the old address."

"Yes," I said, "they had to leave after the Russians kidnapped your uncle."

"Hist, be careful!" He looked around anxiously. "You are in the Eastern sector, not your own."

"On your ground, in fact," I said.

"Yes, on my ground," he said, looking straight at me. "I suppose that in your sector I am still wanted, but Fritz Altmann doesn't exist any more."

"He does," I said sternly. "You can never run away from the past—you'll find that out as you get older. Your sister has found it out already."

"Ursula?" he said.

I nodded.

"Where is she?" he asked.

I told him she was in America.

"And my mother," he asked, looking away from me. "Where did she die? I was told not in Berlin."

I told him where she died.

"Alone?" he asked, with a tremor in his voice.

"No, I was with her," I said. "She died in a strange place, and with none of her family there, and she had suffered terribly, physically as well as mentally."

He kept his face averted.

I said: "She left a message for you, and I promised to give it to you should I ever see you. I never expected to—it's extraordinary—but life *is* extraordinary."

He said, still not looking at me: "Was she very upset that I am a Communist? Did she know?"

I told him that we had known, and that we knew the name he had assumed. He was astounded.

"Oh yes. We are not so stupid over in our Zone," I assured him. "But don't worry, no one is interested in you."

"They couldn't do a thing if they were," he retorted hotly.

"Now, now," I said gently. "Let's leave that out of it. I want to give you your mother's message, and then we will go," and I repeated Frau Altmann's words to him.

He was silent.

I said: "It is only three years since we first met in Berlin, and in that time your father, your sister Lilli, and now your mother have died. Think it over—that's all."

I got up to go. Max hadn't addressed one word to Fritz after giving him a cigarette, but now he said tersely: "I don't give a damn for your politics, rotten as they are, but for the way you treated your mother, whom I loved as my own, I'd like to knock you down, and by God I'm going to."

With a sudden upper-cut he felled Fritz to the ground.

I was appalled at our danger. We were here in the forbidden East sector. If there were a brawl we would both be arrested. Fritz could have us both removed now if he said the word. Too late I thought of my own little one waiting for me at home. Too late I remembered Stampie's warning about Max's unreliability. Fritz was struggling to his feet. His face was contorted with fury, his mouth bleeding.

"Want some more, comrade?" sneered Max.

"Stop it! Stop it!" I cried urgently, and remembering some advice in a book on etiquette for young Victorian women which had said that when in an emergency and at a loss what to do, a lady could always faint, I slithered limply between their feet.

When I got up again there were many interested spectators.

The two were both solicitous and apologetic.

"That was unfair of you, Max," I said, as they helped me to my feet, "and what's more it was very stupid."

Fritz was looking anxiously round at the onlookers.

"I can't fight you here," he said in a low furious voice to Max, "because of our British friend. It would cause trouble for her, and you should know better than to expose her to such danger in a crowd like this. You may not believe me, but I respect her for her own sake, apart from what she has done for my mother. You'd better get out while you can. We'll meet again and I'll pay you back for this."

"I'll escort you to the Tor," Fritz said, taking my arm. "And thank you for coming. I realize what a risk you took to get through such a mob. Isn't it wonderful? It is a huge success."

He took me through the Soviet sentries at the Tor, and bade me goodbye.

"Please believe that, although you can't understand, I loved my mother too, and I *am* grateful to you. What I have done I had to do; there was no other way for me." The sincerity in his voice was too real to be mistaken.

"I believe you," I said, "but for God's sake, Fritz, do you realize where you are going?"

"We are building a new world," he said, throwing out his arms, "and I am going with it. The old one is finished, rotten and worn out. The new one lies before us."

He held out his hand. "I am doing what I believe to be right."

I shook hands, and looked into his face. Now that he was not wearing his Party mask of anticipation and alertness, it was still that of a bewildered little boy.

Max had already withdrawn and was waiting for me through the Tor. We went back to the West sector without a word and joined some friends there.

"I am sorry," he apologized later; "I am terribly ashamed of myself, but when I saw how utterly callous he was about Tante Maria I just had to hit him."

"But he wasn't callous," I corrected him. "There were tears in his eyes when I told him about her death. That's why he kept his face averted. He was totally unprepared for your blow because he was so upset."

"Crocodile tears!" sneered Max. "Haven't you discovered how sentimental we are? Ach! it makes me sick!"

Stampie was very angry indeed when he heard about the whole affair.

"Told you so!" he reminded me. "There's two kinds of Jerries—the one who doesn't think and is a sheep—he's easy to know—and the one who thinks, and he's the kind who turns into the one the others follow. You can never tell with a chap like Max. He's too damn fond of hitting people—it's about time I knocked him out myself."

I told him that it had really been my fault, that the crowd hysteria must have affected me too, because I had suddenly been seized with that violent decision to reach Fritz at all costs, and that the terrible struggle with the mob had been too much for Max, who had just about had enough before he met Fritz.

"I came and looked for you, but in that mass of silly hyp-notized sheep there wasn't a hope, so I went and had some schnapps and looked at it from a distance, and that's the proper place from which to look at such things," said Stampie severely.

The day after my return to Westphalia I saw my son playing in the garden with five other little boys. Four of them were Germans and included his great friend, Hans Jurgen. They were doing some kind of drill and were carrying a flag. They all had toy weapons. One of the young farmers came by in a large wagon.

"Anyone want a ride?" he called.

With shrieks of joy they dropped their things and scrambled up into the farm wagon. I went out and picked up the flag thrown down with the mock guns. It was a swastika, extremely well drawn and painted on a piece of unbleached linen.

EPILOGUE

AUTUMN

1953

It was in an outwardly very different Berlin that Ursula was awaiting me on a lovely September afternoon, and as the plane bringing me from Hanover circled low over the city the new roofs were flashing in the sun. It was exactly the same time of year as when I had come here seven years ago.

Germany was emerging like a great phoenix from her ashes, and here, as in the West, was the sound of the workmen's hammers as they toiled unceasingly to rebuild their cities. There was something frightening in the speed of this re-birth of a defeated nation—just as there was that which compelled one's admiration and praise.

Great blocks of flats, shops, theatres, cinemas and schools were proudly pointed out to me. Flags flew everywhere, the new Federal German one, and the city's standard with its coat of arms, the black bear rampant with a mural crown. The Industrial Exhibition had filled the town with visitors.

I wondered what Ursula would think of her birthplace, which she had not seen for five years. She had left it a grey ruin, and from her letters still regarded it as such. Now she was here, after all this time, and waiting for me at her hotel.

I walked down the Kurfürstendamm and marvelled at its opulence and at the cars parked all down each side of the crowded pavements. At the end of all this new luxury the lovely Gedächtniskirche stood aloof and somehow far more distinguished in its forlorn beauty than any of the slightly vulgar modern buildings. Against a sky streaked with rose from the late sun its grace was that of a lily amongst gaudy sunflowers.

On just such an evening as this Stampie had first pointed it out to me. "Makes a lovely ruin, doesn't it?" he had said whimsically. I was thinking of this as I turned away, and walked back up the Kurfürstendamm to Ursula's hotel.

She was waiting for me there. She had grown into a very lovely woman—and she was beautifully dressed. I had forgotten how young she was as she flung herself impulsively upon me—just as she used to do—and embracing me warmly pulled me down into the chair beside hers. Her voice was a soft drawl, slightly husky, infinitely more attractive than the harsh pseudo-American one she had simulated when last I had seen her.

"You haven't changed a bit!" she cried happily, pulling off her gloves, throwing back her coat, and shaking out her beautiful hair as impetuously as she always did.

But she had—outwardly at least. She was perfectly groomed, her hands white and beautifully manicured, and she wore exquisite shoes and stockings. She had the poise of a woman who is loved and cherished.

We went up to her room. She had a private bathroom and there were flowers everywhere.

"Joe sent those, through the international service. Wasn't it darling of him?" she said, flinging her hat and coat on the bed and pulling some photographs out of her bag.

"I expect you wonder why I'm staying here, and not in the old home—Tante Luise has two lodgers, you know—I'm glad I'm in a hotel; seeing the old place last night upset me. Joe thought it might, that's why he fixed me up here. Here are the children, look, Junior and little Lilli."

"How's Joe?" I asked, examining the snapshots of two laughing children by a swimming pool. The boy was an unmistakable miniature Joe, and the little girl even at this tender age so like Lilli that I caught my breath.

"She has the same very pale gold hair, and the tiniest hands and feet," said Ursula when I remarked on the likeness.

"And Joe?" I asked again.

"He's fine! Getting fat!" she smiled; "he just dotes on Junior and Lilli; you wouldn't have thought he'd make such a good father, would you?"

There were photographs of her typical well-to-do home, and of a charming woman holding Lilli.

"And you get on well with your mother-in-law?" I asked.

"She's a very fine person. We get along splendidly. Mother and I have always understood one another very well."

"Mother," I thought. Ursula must like her very much to call her that. Presently she spoke of her own mother; but with none of the ease with which she discussed her mother-in-law.

"Isn't it a strange thing," she remarked later, "when one becomes a mother oneself things change—I mean, the things I did myself I wouldn't like my Lilli to do. I'd hate it. Isn't that funny? But it's true. I understand now so much better how Mutti must have felt—and how I must have hurt her."

We talked about Tante Luise, whom Ursula had come over to fetch back to the States with her. Stampie had come to Cologne to tell me about Hermann's death on the last occasion I had seen him. Stampie never let us know when he was coming, and we had been on leave in Austria on his subsequent visit and had missed him. He was running a carrier's business with Hermann's friend; they operated four lorries between Berlin, Hamburg, Hanover and Düsseldorf. It was, he told me, money for jam, their profit being a mark per kilometre. He had, of course, taken the dangerous Berlin run for himself. He never wrote letters but he sent me cryptic messages by the drivers of the lorries. There existed a kind of freemasonry between these lorry drivers on the long autobahn runs, and they had related some of Stampie's adventures on the Russian corridor. They would fill a book—he and his cat Lenin had become a legend. "I would so love to have seen him," said Ursula; "he was a grand guy."

The old house, No. 13, in its once lovely garden, looked neglected and dreary when I went there with Ursula. She stood looking up at those twisted iron girders, their nakedness more apparent amongst the new building all round. I wondered if she was remembering how she and Lilli had remained hidden up there from the Russian troops.

Tante Luise was sitting in the chair in which Frau Altmann had always sat. She was darning her lodger's socks. No longer such a frightened little rabbit, her face was bright with the excitement of her niece's visit and the anticipation of returning with her to the States.

She chattered away to me, asking hundreds of questions about my family and our doings, and then told me all the latest talk in Berlin. Had I heard about the uprising of the East workers on June 17th? I had heard of little else from my friends since my arrival. Every Berliner spoke with awe and fear of those terrible days of anguished anxiety when they had heard the shots and seen the fires through the Brandenburger Tor. What had happened once could happen again, and they had been unpleasantly awoken again to the uncertainty of their very existence in their island town. The Red Flag over the ill fated Tor had again been torn down and burned with all the pictures and photographs of Lenin and Stalin by the desperate and furious mob. I should not be taken in by the gay façade of the new buildings, she said; underneath there was still a grim and tense battle.

Ursula had been very silent all this time, but she was listening. She had been very quiet since her return from the camp in the Hohenzollernplatz, where her aunt Karin and her two children were now living. Her eyes went round the old sitting-room, looking at the battered chairs and at the same old pink lampshades—and then at her mother's old sewing machine by the window. Presently she went to the cabinet on the wall and took out a tiny Dresden china dolls' tea-set.

"Lilli and I used to play for hours with this," she said, fingering the tiny cups. "I shall take it back to my Lilli."

The Kurfürstendamm was brilliantly lit and crowded with people as we went back, but there were beggars everywhere—refugees with whom the city was overflowing. It was easy to tell the East people from the West. One look was enough. Ursula stopped and gave money to several, and I was amused to hear how halting her German had become. There were many prostitutes in the shadows, and when I stopped to speak to two of them who were obviously refugees too, Ursula averted her face and walked on.

When I caught her up she burst out in her impulsive way, "I couldn't live here any more! I couldn't live here again! I'm American now in thought and feeling. My children are American, thank God. They won't have to grow up in this terrible, terrible city, still cut into four quarters like an orange. I'm glad, glad, GLAD that I chose a new country!"

She was near to tears as she told me that she had been horribly upset at finding that her young cousin Heinz had been indoctrinated with Communist ideals by her brother Fritz.

Joe's sister was willing to adopt the boy or the girl Rosalia, but Heinz had refused to go to what he considered to be a capitalist country. "I hate Fritz!" she cried bitterly; "there is no end to the harm he has done to that boy—and probably to hundreds of others."

Her aunt Karin had been dispirited and discouraged at not having received a permit to be flown to the West, where she hoped that Heinz would forget his Communist ideals. They had been in the camp for "unrecognized" refugees for over seven months now.

"It's too late to do anything with Heinz; he is fourteen," said Ursula angrily, "and Fritz has been deliberately influencing him for the last three years. I wish Joe was here, he would know better what to do about it."

She was thoroughly upset and depressed.

"Go to bed," I suggested; "you are tired, and visiting old scenes has brought back unhappy memories."

"If it has, they must go back in the cupboard where I keep my skeletons." she replied tersely.

On the evening before the funeral of Professor Ernst Reuter, Berlin's beloved Burgomaster, we were sitting in the café in the Reichskanzlerecke where we had so often sat before. Two American friends of Ursula's were with us. The city was very silent—stunned by the sudden death of this man who had fought so valiantly for its freedom.

"There is no one to follow him," said the Berliners, whose faces wore the tense look of not knowing what comes next. "He was the only one who really cared about our city's future. What will happen to us now?" And they pointed to the black bears on the standards. "Poor bear," they said; "he must dance to every tune."

In every window round us burned a candle for the dead man, who had introduced the lighting of one for every German still missing in Russia. Now the Berliners burned them for him.

Ursula's friends left us to greet some acquaintances, and Ursula who had been very quiet suddenly asked me about Max. Had I heard from him lately?

I had been dreading having to tell her that Max was in prison. Influenced doubtless by his uncle in Bavaria, who was a member of the Naumann group, Max had become interested in the Frei Deutschland Korps, and had been arrested in the unexpected swoop the Federal Government had made on the party in the early part of the year. He was due to be released shortly, no specific charge having been preferred against most of them. Stampie had first told me of his Nazi activities. He and Max had quarrelled violently about it. When Stampie had said that it was childish to go on playing at Nazis when Hitler was dead and extreme right wing politics a thing of the past, Max had shouted that Christ was dead but that there were still millions of Christians. What could you do with a man like that? asked the bewildered Stampie.

Ursula was incredulous, and could not believe it at first. Then she asked, with two brilliant spots of colour in her cheeks, "Hasn't he married that Austrian girl?"

I told her that, according to Stampie, Max's whole heart was in the Nazi revival. I remembered his words, "Whatever I do, I do with my whole heart." Stampie was probably right. In any case Max had not married and did not appear to be interested in women.

"He must be mad to go on with that ridiculous rubbish," cried Ursula. "I would never have believed it of him."

She had obviously received a severe shock, and when her friends rejoined us she tried in vain to resume her naturally gay manner. Suddenly she cried violently:

"Let's have some drinks—anything to forget this terrible, terrible city with all these refugees—and Heinz, and now Max. I can't get over it."

The waiter brought the drinks.

"Well, what shall this one be?" asked one of her young friends, as he held up his glass.

"To Berlin!" cried the other before we could speak. We drank to the city's future freedom—and all round us the little lights twinkled for the dead Burgomaster whose coffin would be carried on the morrow past that great Russian tank on the Potsdamer Chaussée to the lovely Wald cemetery.

I was suddenly aware that Ursula was weeping bitterly. Tears were pouring down her cheeks unchecked as she put her head down on the table and sobbed. Her friends were concerned and embarrassed, thinking that she was overcome by the melancholy of the whole atmosphere.

"Leave her alone," I whispered; "it will do her good to cry a little," for I realized at that moment that the orchestra which had been playing the waltz theme from *Moulin Rouge* was now beginning to play very softly the *Rhapsody in Blue*, which Ursula loved so much and which they had played all through her wedding party.

We went outside into the cool air and I looked at the Square where I had first met her mother, now an elegant place with the latest traffic signals. There were trees and flowers in the centre where once guarded prisoners had cleared away debris. I looked at the black bears on the standards fluttering in the breeze and thought of the Berliners' words about the bear having to dance to so many tunes. The German tune would now be added to the other four; the Federal Government was no longer a puppet one and Dr Adenauer was making his voice heard about an independent Germany.

I turned to find Ursula beside me. She was quite calm, although her face was tear-stained. She made no attempt to wipe away the wet marks and looked very young and vulnerable.

"It's over," she said, slipping her arm through mine, and in her tremulous smile there was now something of her mother's courage. We stood there together for a long time looking at all the little lights.

THE END

The following sketches were made by Frances Faviell while she lived in Berlin between 1946 and 1949. They have never before been published, and appear now courtesy of Frances Faviell's son, John Parker

Lunden

dead sister
'40

AFTERWORD

I THINK I was about 11 when I realised my mother was becoming a writer as well as being a painter. I was home from my English boarding school for the summer holidays when my father suggested that I should not disturb my mother in the mornings as she would be working. ... At the time I was upset as my mother had never seemed to worry if I disturbed her.

My mother was born and grew up in Plymouth, Devon. She was the fourth of five surviving children born to Anglo Scottish parents. Named Olive, she showed her innate independence at an early age by insisting she be called Olivia. She showed early talent as an artist and in her late teens won a scholarship to the Slade School of Art, then still under the direction of Henry Tonks. Her tutor, and later good friend, at the school was the painter Leon Underwood.

In 1930 she married her first husband, a Hungarian academic, whose work took him to first Holland and then India. But they separated while there (and later divorced). She then stayed on for three months in the Ashram of the great Indian thinker and writer Rabindranath Tagore. Travelling on her own, painting and sketching, she visited other parts of India including Assam and for a few weeks lived with the Nagas, a primitive indigenous people in northeast India. On her way back to England she travelled via Japan and then China – still painting and sketching – until she had to flee Shanghai when the Japanese invaded.

On her return to England she lived in Chelsea, then a haven for artists, and earned her living as a portrait painter. She met my father, who had recently resigned from the Indian Civil Service, in 1939, and they were married in 1940 after he had joined the Ministry of Information. Bombed out during the Blitz, as portrayed in her last book, *A Chelsea Concerto*, they spent the rest of the war, after I was born, in the Home Counties before returning to Chelsea in 1945.

When the war ended my father was recruited to the Control Commission of Germany and became a high ranking official in the British administration, first in Berlin, negotiating with the others of the four powers on the organisation of the city, later in the British zone of West Germany.

We joined him in Berlin in early 1946 and it was here that my mother encountered the Altmann family. It was her experiences with them that inspired her to start writing her first book, *The Dancing Bear*, which movingly describes Berlin in defeat through the eyes of the defeated as well as the victors.

Each of her books, whether non-fiction or fiction, were inspired by an episode in her own life. By 1951 we had moved to Cologne and it was here that her second book, the novel *A House on the Rhine,* was conceived, based around migrant families (from the east of Germany) she had met and helped.

Subsequently, she published another novel, *Thalia*, based on her own experience in France before the War when she was acting as a chaperone to a young teenager for the summer. Her final novel *The Fledgeling*, about a National Service deserter, was also based on an actual incident.

My mother was diagnosed with breast cancer in 1956 though I did not know at the time. At first radiotherapy seemed to have arrested the disease. But then two years later, it reappeared. She fought the disease with courage and humour, exhibiting the same clear sightedness with which she had viewed life around her as a painter and a writer. She died just after *A Chelsea Concerto* was published, in 1959.

In her books as in her life, my mother had an openness to and compassion for others and, when she saw an injustice or need, would not be thwarted by authority of any kind in getting something done. But as she always pursued her causes with charm as well as firmness, few could deny her requests for long.

John Richard Parker, 2016

FURROWED MIDDLEBROW

Manufactured by Amazon.ca
Bolton, ON

26615253R00129